THE HEART OF HEALING

THE HEART OF HEALING

A Handbook on Healing

by

GEORGE BENNETT

Author of

Miracle at Crowhurst
In His Healing Steps
Commissioned to Heal

ARTHUR JAMES LIMITED
ONE CRANBOURNE ROAD, LONDON N10 2BT

DEDICATION

To

My Wife

A TRIBUTE FROM
HIS GRACE
THE ARCHBISHOP OF YORK

I WELCOME this book, because I believe it will help forward that healing ministry of the Church which is surely part of its function today as it was in the early days.

I welcome it for its sanity and for the strong pastoral sense by which it is marked throughout. May it be widely read.

DONALD EBOR:

1971

PREFACE

THE CHURCH is happily recovering her healing ministry today. The old incredulity and suspicion have gone. Clergy and laity alike are seeing it afresh as an integral part of the Church's total gospel. The questions they are asking today are of a positive nature: "Are all the clergy called to minister healing?" "Is it necessary to have a special gift?" "What part can the layman play?" "Must you have faith before you can be healed?" "How should we pray for healing?" "What about doctors and nurses?" These are among the many questions they are asking and which this book seeks to answer. I have tried to bring together some of the thoughts I have been privileged to express about them when lecturing and conducting missions of healing, and which clergy and other friends have kindly encouraged me to put into print. I am very grateful for this encouragement and also for the immense help that my publishers have given me.

If what I have written can be accepted as a small contribution to current thinking about this ministry I shall be more than grateful.

A new Church is emerging today amidst the erosion of the old patterns dominated for many centuries by European Christianity. She is being reshaped by the Holy

Spirit and being brought into closer kinship with the primitive Christian Church than she has been at any time in the intervening centuries.

As I travel in this country and abroad, I am continually seeing exciting evidence of this phenomenon taking place. House groups and prayer-and-care groups, which cut through denominational barriers, are among them. And clergy tell me that since accepting the healing ministry and integrating it into their total awareness of what the Church is called to be and do, their whole theology has been transformed and brought meaningfully alive.

Increasingly I have found that the ministry of healing involves the whole Church and not necessarily the clergy alone. Indeed it seems to bring lay people more into an active purposeful membership than any other aspect of her life and witness. It is for this reason I often use the wider term "ministrant" or "helper". Except for the administration of the Sacraments a ministrant can be any layman who believes in the healing work of Christ.

The new Church which is emerging sees once again that her Lord's command is two-fold: "Preach the kingdom and heal the sick." This realisation is not the product of human minds. It is a "happening", a shaping by the Holy Spirit.

Where I have used Bible quotations they have been taken from the Revised Version or the Revised Standard Version unless otherwise stated.

GEORGE BENNETT

CONTENTS

I

THREE QUESTIONS

I WONDER IF the most decisive moments come when we least expect them? I think this is generally true of my own life. Certainly I never expected anything out of the ordinary to happen on that bright summer afternoon, now so many years ago.

The occasion was serious enough as it was, for I was setting out to call on a sick parishioner. But I did not reckon on the vital consequences that particular visit would have for me and for the whole of my future ministry.

I had only just heard of his illness. He was a sidesman of our church and very popular. The news had come to me only by chance and I wished I had known earlier, for apparently he had been in bed a few days. My informant wasn't sure what the trouble was. All she could tell me was that a specialist had been called.

I knew he suffered with his heart and I wondered, as I got near to his home, if there had been a sudden collapse.

In answer to my ring, his wife opened the door. I told her I had only just heard of her husband's illness and asked if I could come in.

For a moment she did not reply. Then she shook her head.

"I am sorry," she managed to say at last, "but I can't let you in! I daren't let anybody in."

Her lips trembling, she managed to tell me that the doctors had only just left the house and were going to send a nurse as soon as possible. In the meantime, he was not to be disturbed by anybody at all.

She told me that the trouble was pneumonia and it had got worse over the past three days. The crisis would come in a day or two and I wondered, with his weak heart, if he could survive. Pneumonia was a killer disease in those days. The healing properties of penicillin had not been discovered.

"Can't I just say a prayer with him?" I asked. "I will be very quiet."

But she was adamant. We were good friends and I knew she was finding it hard to refuse me.

I turned away from the house, deeply troubled. I was anxious enough, as it was, for this woman and her very sick husband, but something troubled me even more. When Christ was on earth, I managed to tell myself, He would have been welcomed at such a house as this. But today His followers, His representatives, are not wanted. They might make things worse!

I wondered what had happened to the Church that still bore His name. What, in this twentieth century, had it become? And what, therefore, was my ordination all about?

I was serving a curacy in this parish and had been ordained only three years before. My call to the ministry had come out of a conversion experience when, as a medical student, I had been an agnostic. Christ had turned my life upside down. I knew He could do wonderful things. What might happen even to this situation were He to be let right into the heart of it!

Sometimes, at theological college, I had raised the matter of the Church's ministry of healing during lectures and sometimes I had introduced the subject at our late evening discussions in each other's rooms, but my questionings had usually been rebuffed. Faith-healing they called it then, and I was told "we do not approve of that"! The only advice I could get was to read large books about the "problem of suffering".

So, like most young parsons, I had simply accepted the sick-visiting list that my vicar gave me each week at our staff meetings and I called faithfully and regularly on those whose names and addresses were there. Always I tried to bring some measure of comfort to help them find patience under their sufferings, and wherever possible I would conclude my visit with a short prayer and perhaps the reading of a few well-known verses from the Bible.

But when I left them I was strangely uneasy. Vaguely, I felt that something vital had been left out. Though it was encouraging to hear the thanks of the relatives and to be assured that my visit had brought comfort, I knew in my heart that there was much more that I ought to have been able to give.

But here was a house which I could not even enter, let alone say a prayer. The man was too ill!

Suddenly I felt lost. I seemed to be entering into a deep, dark wood.

I walked and kept on walking through the streets of that parish for the next two hours or so. Possibly I passed folk who knew me. I don't know. Certainly I could not have greeted them except in a very absent-minded way.

It seemed as though my whole ministry was at stake.

I do not know when the first question came. I had been walking a long time when it did. Suddenly it came into my consciousness like a bolt from the blue.

It was followed, after a long interval, by a second question and a third, and I knew that to each one I had to give a definite answer. There was a sense of finality about them. It was as if I were being asked them then, once for all, and that there would never in this lifetime be another chance to find the answers.

I know now that these three questions did not come simply from my subconscious mind. They had their origin outside of me.

The first question was, "Do I really believe that when Christ was on earth He really healed people?"

Strange that such a question should come to me, for I had never doubted it; but instinctively I knew that I had to ponder the question afresh as though I had never heard it before nor ever would again.

"*Do I really believe that when Christ was on earth He really healed people?*"

Conversations we had at college came flooding back into my mind. I remembered lectures where it was generally accepted that though He did indeed heal people, His healing works were for that particular age, the messianic age, alone. Then again, someone had likened His healing works to the sound of a great bell calling people's attention so that they would come and listen. His teaching, they said, was what really mattered.

Some of the books I had read seemed to suggest that there was a measure of folk-lore written into the gospels and that His healing works came under this heading. Others thought that they could be explained by modern psychology.

I had heard preachers proclaim that these stories of healing were to be accepted not so much at their face value but rather because of the deeper spiritual truths that they conveyed.

All these thoughts and memories came rushing back and I turned them over in my mind afresh, giving weight to each one. Some of them, I thought, contained a little bit of truth, but all put together fell far short of the whole truth. They raised too many other problems. The question that had come to me now kept ringing in my mind. I had to give a clear yea or nay.

"Do I really believe that when Christ was on earth He really healed people?"

I gave my answer.

I did not know that a second question was to follow. I still felt the dark wood about me. After a while it came:

"Do I really believe that after they killed Him—and they did kill Him when they crucified Him—He really rose again?"

Again I thought of lectures I had heard, discussions I had joined in, books and articles by eminent thinkers I had read about the subject of the resurrection. These were the days of the "modernists" and various interpretations were being given to the meaning of Christ's resurrection. It may be, some explained, that it was to be seen in the birth of the Church. His own bodily rising did not matter.

These thoughts, too, I considered afresh as I let the question go round and round in my mind. In the end, though, I knew the answer had to be my own. No matter what the most learned professor in all the world might believe, *"do I really believe that after they killed Him He really rose again?"*

I gave my answer.

The third and final question came only a short time afterwards.

"*Do I really believe that He is the same, yesterday, today and forever?*"

There were no theories about this, as far as I could remember, but I knew that I had to give a clear and definite answer and that no one else could give it for me. In a few moments I gave it and, as I did so, a wonderful sense of peace descended on me. It was as though I had left the dark wood behind me and had arrived home.

I found myself walking back to the house and I rang the bell again. The door opened and the sick man's wife was standing there once more. She thought it was the nurse arriving but when she saw me standing there she just stood back from the door and let me in. With only a smile I went past her and climbed the stairs, seeking her husband's room. Many years later I asked her if I had been rude on that occasion in pushing past her like that and she told me, "No, some Power prevented me from doing or saying anything. I knew you had to do what you had to do."

I shall always remember his room. The curtains were drawn and it came back to me that, despite my dark wood, it was still a bright summer day. I suppose they were drawn to ease the pressure of light on his eyes. But the greatest thing about that room—the breath-taking thing—was that it was full of the power of the living Christ.

As I crossed the room to kneel at the man's bedside, a naively simple thought came into my mind: the Power is here, all about us, and all He wants is someone to pull down the switch.

The sick man was lying on his back, leaning slightly against the pillows, and I felt I ought to be touching him. As I did so, he raised his hand under the coverlet and I took it in mine. After a moment I spoke a prayer, the kind of prayer that any child could say. I asked our blessed Lord to fill him with divine power, to drive away the illness and to heal him.

I was not there long and as I got up to leave him, he turned his face towards me and, with a smile, he said, "Thank you, George, I will be all right now. Tell my wife, won't you?"

She was still standing in the hall where I had left her.

"He will be all right now," I said to her as I went out.

And, wonderfully, so it turned out to be! In a few hours her husband was sitting up in bed. In a few days he was out and about again. The illness dispersed. No crisis ever came.

In the years that followed we became great friends. I shall always treasure the beautifully engraved silver napkin ring he gave me when I left that parish. Even more shall I remember with gratitude the look he gave me following his recovery. We looked into each other's eyes as if we had shared the certain knowledge that Christ is indeed alive yesterday, today and forever, and wanting to work through His Church as ever He did of old.

Over the years since that day I have seen many wonderful things happening in the lives of many people. Men and women whose lives have been broken by the harshness of this world have been given release and a new happiness, and many have been healed.

But I often look back to what happened to me that particular summer afternoon and I thank God because it pointed me along a journey which has led into the heart of all healing—the wholeness that comes from knowing, in every part of one's being, the love of Christ.

II

RECOVERY OF A LOST DIMENSION

IN THESE DAYS the Church is, happily, recovering her healing ministry, yet there are still good Christians who regard divine healing as something which is not really necessary to the everyday life of a church. They agree that it might perhaps concern some individuals, like hospital chaplains, and that there may also be others who by their nature are specially called in that direction.

I can understand this attitude. Following my conversion experience my training for the ministry was via the evangelical branch of the Church. The greatest thing in my life was the saving power of the gospel. Christ had changed my life and I knew He could change the lives of others. That was what I wanted to preach, what I wanted the whole world to know. Why complicate this glorious message with healing?

But right from the beginning I had a deep intuitive feeling that if the gospel were to be preached in all its fullness Christ's work of healing could not be left out. Until that afternoon when I had set out to visit a sick man and had been turned away this feeling had never really been challenged. True, there had been pointers here and there, like signposts along the road, but I had never looked for any great significance in them. Now, they were coming back to my mind.

I have already spoken of my visiting the sick people on my list. Did it mean anything when relatives told me that they were feeling better as a result of those visits when we had spent together a little time of prayer?

Then there had been the occasion when, as with most clergy, I had been called out to baptise a dying baby and had often heard later that the baby had recovered.

There was the strange incident of the old lady who lived with her married daughter and her family on the outskirts of a new housing area at the far end of our large parish. My vicar had given me special responsibility for this area and, following an urgent phone call from the old lady's daughter, had kindly driven me out to see her. He waited for me while I went inside.

The daughter told me that it was unlikely that her mother would survive the week-end. She had telephoned the vicar immediately after the doctor had called. She took me upstairs and left me there.

I sat at the old lady's bedside and, after a little while, opened my New Testament at the fourteenth chapter of St. John's Gospel.

"Let not your heart be troubled," I read the words slowly to her, "ye believe in God, believe also in me. In my Father's house are many mansions. . . ."

This is a passage of great beauty and has brought comfort to many. They are the words of Jesus spoken to His twelve disciples in the intimacy of the Upper Room on the night before He was crucified. I turn invariably to this passage when visiting someone who is dying. I intended to read as far as the ninth verse where Jesus says, "He that hath seen Me hath seen the Father."

As I approached this verse, however, there suddenly came to me the strange conviction that the old lady was not going to die. At least, not at that time. It was a conviction that came quite unexpectedly and I wanted time to think about it. So, instead of finishing my reading at the ninth verse I continued on to the next and finally read the whole chapter. By this time I felt that the prayer I had originally intended to use was out of place and I said some other instead.

I told my vicar as I rejoined him in his car that I did not think she was going to die and, sure enough, she didn't! She recovered and lived happily for another two years or so. Her daughter and her family were profoundly affected and became active supporters of our church.

This experience has always remained a mystery to me but, at the time, I wondered if perhaps a power of healing had entered into the life of that old lady during the reading of those lovely words.

So my mind went round and round, recalling little incidents here and there. I had no one to guide me but that, perhaps, was just as well, for I had to find my own way for awhile. There was nothing concrete to go on. Other and more down-to-earth explanations could have been given to these few experiences. After all, I was still very young in the ministry. But I still felt there were things here that could not be entirely explained away. There was a touch of heaven's mystery about them.

Now, in a deep and dramatic way I had been challenged. Three questions had come to me and I had given my answers to them. There could be no going back. I was having to re-think all I had been taught at my theological college and to look again at the Book of Common Prayer and especially at my New Testament. Through the years that have gone since that summer afternoon I have realised that those three questions have been the dominating force of my life.

Yet my love of the gospel which meant so much to me then has not changed. Rather, it has deepened. It has become filled with a whole new dimension.

Let me put it this way:

I have at home a few books on famous art. One day I take one of them down from the shelves and slowly turn the pages. On each page is a copy in black and white of a well-known picture by a famous artist. Eventually I arrive at a page where a certain picture compels my attention. I want to look no further. This picture holds me; it fascinates me and I am at peace with it. I don't want to turn the pages any more.

Then, a few days later, I find myself in a strange town and with time to spare. I slip into an art gallery and after a little while I find myself confronted with my picture. I stand and gaze at it. It is the same but it is different. It is full of colour and the colours in it give a depth that my copy at home lacks. It seems to have another dimension. This is the original picture as the artist created it and intended it to be.

My picture at home, though it satisfied me at the time, I realise now, had something vitally important missing. A whole dimension!

So I began to look again at the things I had come to love—our church services, the Bible, my own prayers, all that I had been taught of the Christian faith.

Phrases we had always used began to have a new significance. "Thy saving health unto all nations" and the words we used every Sunday morning and evening during the General Confession: "We have erred and strayed from thy ways like lost sheep . . . *and there is no health in us.*" I began to see that there was a greater depth in our Holy Communion Service than I had previously realised. It could be glimpsed in such phrases as "Preserve *thy body* and soul unto everlasting life" and "all other benefits of His passion". It seemed that we entered here not simply into a service that was good for our souls but also into the very heart of all creation.

The phrase "if it be Thy will" in the prayer for the sick just had to go! Goodness knows what would happen to our prayer life and to our faith if we inserted these words into every prayer we offered!

Instead of saying "Let us pray for the sick" I found myself saying, "Let us pray for the healing of the sick." It seemed to deepen and give more intention to the purpose of the prayer.

I came to realise that as far as the Bible is concerned health and salvation are inseparable. The two go together. The phrase in St. James's Epistle can be translated "the prayer of faith shall *save* the sick" or "the prayer of faith shall *heal* the sick". It is we, in our materialistic western world, who have separated the two.

Furthermore, the Bible sees man as an essential whole. The division we have made for so long between body, mind and spirit is not the message of Holy Scripture. It stems from the Graeco-Roman philosophic thought on which so much of our civilisation is built.

It seemed to me that when our Lord addressed Himself to the needs of those who came to Him He saw them as whole people, not just as souls to be saved, not just as sick people with bodies to be healed. He saw sickness as well as sin as being the result of what we call "the fall". He came to bring wholeness. It did not matter whether or not He said to the man sick of the palsy, "Son, thy sins be forgiven thee"—a spiritual matter, or "Take up thy bed and walk"—a physical matter. He came to set the man free from all that harmed and hurt him.

When He went into the synagogue right at the beginning of His ministry and was invited to speak to the assembled congregation He chose specially for His reading a passage from Isaiah, the theme of which was just this. He could have chosen some other passage. There were plenty that had to do with the eventual coming of the Messiah and of the need for repentance when He came. The passage He chose was more gracious than these:

"The Spirit of the Lord is upon Me, because He hath anointed Me to preach good tidings to the poor: He hath sent Me to proclaim release to the captives, and recovering of sight to the blind, to set at liberty them that are bruised, to proclaim the acceptable year of the Lord."

This was the proclamation of what His ministry was to be all about!

Almost immediately people began to bring their sick ones to Him and He healed them all.

If this work of healing worries people now, it certainly worried them then! Even John the Baptist, his forerunner, was taken aback. He could not understand and began to have his doubts about Jesus. From his prison cell he sent two messengers to ask Jesus: "Art thou he that should come or look we for another?"

And how telling was the unspoken answer Jesus gave him:

"In that hour He healed many of diseases and plagues and evil spirits; and on many that were blind He bestowed sight."

He told the messengers to go back and tell John what they had seen. Then, having reported it, they were to say, "Blessed is he who shall find no occasion of stumbling in Me!"

When, as His ministry progressed, He selected from all His disciples twelve who would continue His work, He sent them out on a training mission. He did not tell them just to preach the gospel but rather to proclaim the gospel by the preaching of the kingdom and the healing of the sick. It was clear that He wanted them to continue the work that He did. He would provide the power.

It was a two-fold commission. The preaching and the healing belonged together. They were inseparable.

So began my journey into the world where Christ heals. It was the beginning of an exploration into the deeper dimensions of the gospel which changed my life years ago, and through the years I have found cause to praise God many times for the working of His healing grace in the lives of more men, women and children than I can remember.

I often feel, now, that what we have is not so much a ministry of healing but rather a glorious gospel which is so tremendous that it meets all the needs of man at every point. No one is left out.

III

A WORLD RESTORED

"PREACH THE KINGDOM and heal the sick!" This two-fold commission of our Lord burned more and more deeply into my heart and mind. It expressed so perfectly what He Himself did and if, as I believed then and still believe, He wants His Church to continue His work, this is what we must always be doing.

Whether He preached or whether He healed, the whole gospel was being proclaimed. Preaching and healing go hand in hand. They give significance to each other. To accept and obey one half of the commission and to ignore or deny the other is to empty the half that is accepted of much of its meaning and power.

With Him the two were inseparable aspects of His total work. It seemed to me that it needed no stretch of the imagination to think of people being healed while they were simply listening to His preaching. After all, great preachers have always experienced this kind of happening. John Wesley did. And often have I heard missionaries tell of sudden healings taking place when they have been simply preaching the gospel. There is a power in the gospel message, when preached from the heart, that goes deeply into every part of our beings. And this is immeasurably true when the man who is preaching is one who sets no limit to what the Spirit of God can do. His clear belief and faith is somehow communicated to his hearers, whatever the words he uses.

Similarly, our Lord's healing work was also a preaching. It was a demonstration actually taking place of what the kingdom meant in the lives of those who came to Him seeking help. This, I think, is the significance that lies in the answer that Jesus gave to John the Baptist. "In that hour He healed many . . ."

I began to think what His kingdom might be. I saw it as a world set free from all the powers of evil that are manifested in creation and in the lives of men, where sin and sickness had been overcome and where the divine potentialities inherent in all creation were at last released. I began to look beyond the gospel story of our Lord's preaching and healing work to the underlying fight He waged against what He called "the prince of this world". So I read the gospels afresh.

As I turned the pages I realised I had never before seen quite so clearly what the gospel of our redemption cost Him. It was from first to last the grimmest struggle the world has ever seen—or ever will see. It seemed that right at the outset all the powers of evil were arrayed against His coming into the world, that even as a babe His life was threatened.

And no wonder, I thought, as I read again about the early days of His ministry among us, that it was the evil spirits who were the first to recognise Him. "We know who you are!" they cried out. "Are you come to destroy us?"

He told the scribes and pharisees when they came to accuse Him of healing demented minds by the power of Beelzebub, "If I by the finger of God cast out devils, no doubt the kingdom of God is come upon you!"

Always He saw sin and sickness as enemy invaders, as outward manifestations of the evil which pervades our fallen creation. They belonged, ultimately, to Satan's world. They were to be rebuked, cast out, overcome. They despoiled His Father's creation. Let loose into the world since creation began, they had now met their match.

Jesus came to bring release to the captives. He came to do in man and for man what man could not do for himself. He knew what deliverance meant. He knew what the world would look like were the kingdom of God to come. He could see the world in its perfection even in the midst of all its imperfections. He saw a world restored, with all the powers of sin and sickness brought underfoot. He was completing His Father's work. "I come to do the will of Him that sent Me," He said in explanation of His work. "My Father worketh hitherto and I work."

He had, if we may use ordinary human terms, a passionate jealousy for His Father's work of creation and a hatred of all that despoiled it.

Some years ago a friend showed me over his factory. It had been founded by his father some thirty years earlier. As we walked round the various "shops" he introduced me to some of the men working there. There was a happy atmosphere everywhere we went. Some of them had joined the factory when it had been started by his father and they could remember when it was little more than a shed and there were only thirty or forty of them then. Now it had grown a hundredfold. I could sense the feeling of pride in these men that they should be working there, and this was reflected in my friend's attitude as he showed me round.

Every now and then he would point to a machine and

say, "My father designed that," or, "My father made that." There was no mistaking the warmth of pride and affection he displayed.

As I came out of the factory these phrases continued to ring through my mind. "My father made that!" "My father designed that!" I thought of them as I looked up at the trees growing along the side of the road. I thought of them as I saw men and women going about their daily rounds. Some children were skipping their way home from school. Suddenly I felt I was sharing in the way our Lord looked at us, at the men and women and children who came to Him, at the sparrow in the hedgerow and the lily growing in the field. "My Father made that!" one could hear Him saying to Himself.

No wonder He was angry when the leper said to Him, "If thou wilt, thou canst make me clean." There was all the compassion in the world for the poor man himself but His compassion was tinged with anger not only at the terrible sickness itself but also at the very thought that there was an "If" about what was His will, that there might be any doubt about His desire to release him and make him whole.

Jesus saw this man not only as he was at that moment but also as His Father had intended him to be—whole and happy and living a purposeful life, not just existing in the shadows.

I remember a mother bringing her teenage daughter to see me. She had written asking if I could help. Her daughter, Joanna, was now thirteen and had suffered from a skin disorder since she was six months old. She had been vaccinated at that time and something had gone wrong. Every morning her mother had to sweep from her bed the skin which had fallen off during the night and Joanna herself had to wear cotton next to her skin. She wore cotton gloves and carried a light shawl over her head.

While her mother waited in another room Joanna and I sat down to have a talk together. All I could see of her face, as I looked between the folds of her shawl, were her clear blue eyes, her slightly blotched nose and her lips.

After a little while she told me that despite her trouble she was a teacher in her Sunday School at home. She told me she taught the tiny tots.

"Well, Joanna," I said, "you don't need me to tell you what would happen if we take your sickness to Jesus and ask Him to heal it for you, do you?" Her eyes were smiling as she shook her head.

I said, "Well, let us do that, shall we?"

Joanna knelt and I stood by her. After a few moments' silence while we rested in the surrounding love of God I offered a prayer to our Lord, asking Him to release her from this thing and to fill her with His healing power. Then I turned to Joanna and, making the sign of the Cross over her, I rebuked the illness in the Name of Jesus of Nazareth. I put my hands on her veiled head and prayed that the love of our risen Lord would flood her whole being with His cleansing and healing power.

As she rejoined her mother and we shook hands to go our different ways I asked if she would write to me in about a fortnight's time and let me know how Joanna was.

Two weeks later her letter came. In fact, there were two letters in the envelope, one from Joanna which was quite short and which was very like the kind of letter a child would write to her uncle thanking him for a birthday present, and the other from her mother which told me much more.

Apparently, the disorder had got much worse during the forty-eight hours following the ministration. But then, quite suddenly, areas of new baby skin had begun to appear. These had gradually spread all over her body and now only the extremities of her fingers and feet had any sign of the sickness left.

It is interesting how there is sometimes an initial worsening of the trouble during the day or two following a ministration. It does not happen often, but it had happened in Joanna's case. I call it "the badness coming out".

I asked her mother to bring Joanna to see me again. I wanted to say a thank-you to our Lord with her and to give her a final ministration.

This time the girl looked quite different. Her smiling face was no longer veiled and her fair hair, beautifully reflecting the light, swung loosely from her head. It reminded me of one of those television advertisements one sometimes sees for shampoos! Her skin was clear. The blotches had gone.

There was no need, this time, for a separate little talk, so her mother stayed to kneel at Joanna's side as I led them in a little act of thanksgiving. After I had given another ministration and as we moved to the door her mother asked, "Did you notice her hair?"

"Indeed, I did," I replied, "and isn't it beautiful?"

"I have always told her that one day she would have beautiful hair. Even when she was a little child I knew it would be one day, and she wouldn't believe me. Now she knows!"

As I waved them goodbye I could not help recalling the words of my friend in the factory and I added to myself: "And that is just how our heavenly Father intended her to be!"

Some months later Joanna sent me a studio photograph of herself, the first she had ever had taken. She looked pretty in her new dress, and her mother also wrote to tell me she had bought a swimming costume for her. Until then, Joanna had never been able to join in the games that many of her friends played.

As I looked at the photograph I offered a silent and heartfelt thanksgiving to our Lord that He had set her free and that in her young life His will had been done.

IV

A GIFT OF HEALING

NOWADAYS there is a growing interest in the gifts of the Spirit about which St. Paul writes in the twelfth chapter of his Epistle to the Corinthians. Many want to know especially about the gift of healing, what it means and how it comes.

Looking back to those early days in my own ministry, we thought not so much about a gift as what it was a Christian believed. Had he faith to believe that Christ could heal today as He did of old? And that question is still to me the crux of the whole situation. Have we faith to believe that with God all things are possible? For without that faith none of the gifts of the Spirit will come.

Sometimes we would hear, as we still do, about people who seem to have been born with the gift. Some, indeed, use it on animals as well as on human beings. Sometimes we read a newspaper account of a healer and of the remarkable things that happen, or are claimed to have happened, when sick folk have gone to him after all medical help has failed. A Welsh surgeon once told me that this gift seemed to come especially to members of the Celtic race. He remembered that in his boyhood days there was hardly a village in his country which did not have some inhabitant who had it. Sometimes it was passed from parents to children in one particular family.

Though these things intrigued me then, I was never greatly interested. Far more important to me was the spread of the knowledge of our Lord Jesus Christ. This kind of faith-healing (a phrase I have never liked) seemed to be a phenomenon akin to dowsing. I was looking for something much more worthwhile than that.

Occasionally, however, there were other reports about "healers" which had a quite different "feel" about them. These seemed to indicate that their work flowed from the gospel message. They put the love of God right in the middle of the picture.

About that time there was a layman, James Moore Hickson, whose healing gift was being much used in the recovery by the Church of her healing ministry. He had travelled the world conducting services of healing and had the growing support of many clergy and lay people. The story of his travels read very much like a page from the New Testament. Everywhere he went Christ was glorified. Following his visit to Australia the Bishops there had issued a Pastoral Letter urging the Church everywhere to claim again this long-lost aspect of her total gospel.

"We shall never forget," they wrote, "the wonderful realisation of the presence of our Lord moving amongst the sick . . . with His hands outstretched in blessing. We awoke to the living romance of the gospel in action in our midst . . . Our cathedrals have been happier places ever since."

My heart was warmed and I felt strangely and deeply moved whenever I read or heard about this kind of thing. It encouraged me to go on giving the laying-on-of-hands

34

whenever I felt the Spirit moving me to do so. This ministry was becoming as natural to me as the ministry of the spoken word. But I never felt entirely happy whenever anyone told me they thought that I had a gift of healing. Only One could heal, and that was the risen Christ. We were but instruments in His hands and channels through which His healing love could flow. I have always strongly felt that the healing ministry finds its rightful place only when it is lifted above the level of the individual "healer" into the glory of Christ as seen throughout His Church. It was something that all Christian believers ought to be engaged in.

About five years after that experience on a summer afternoon, I met the man who was to help me more than anyone else. He was Godfrey Mowatt, another layman, who only the day before had been specially commissioned by Archbishop William Temple for this work in the Church.

I was invited, with a few other clergymen, by the then Bishop of Coventry, to go to his house, where Godfrey was staying for a few days. "He has a wonderful gift of healing," the Bishop told me.

As I shook hands with him I was startled to find that he was blind. I wondered why God had not healed him, but this feeling passed very quickly. As Godfrey began to speak I realised that here was a man who was living victoriously in Christ and, as he unfolded his story, I knew that he was more wonderfully whole than any of the rest of us there. His words were simple but full of spiritual power. They spoke to the very depths. I felt that a door was opening wide at the threshold of heaven itself. I think that everyone present felt that we had been transported on to a higher plane. The phrase "the living Christ" that had come ringing from his lips stayed in my mind for a long time.

I got to know Godfrey very well from that day until he passed into what he often called "the wider life". We often shared in conferences and services of healing. Never did he mention a gift of healing. All he wanted to talk about were "the healing mercies" of God and of people's minds and bodies being healed through "the power of the living Christ".

One day he told me how it all had happened. He had lost his sight when he was a small boy cutting a piece of string with a sharp penknife, and the knife had slipped. Later he had other accidents and, in a car-crash a glass eye which he had had fitted split into fragments. Lying in hospital in severe agony and railing against life and God he suddenly heard a still, small voice: "You fool, this railing does neither you nor anyone any good. Hand yourself entirely over to Me and I will use you." From that moment he surrendered everything that he was and had. The pain vanished and he found himself in perfect peace.

"*Hand yourself over to Me.*" Here, I felt, was the clue to the whole situation. How does a gift of the Spirit come? By abandoning ourselves and our own desires in utter surrender and obedience to the Spirit of God, for Him to do with us as He pleases. Whatever we are, God made us; and whatever capabilities we may have, He gave them. All we are and all we have are really His. If we return our gifts to Him Who gave them He makes them His own. He blesses and increases them in us for His glory.

God does not hand out His gifts like a Santa Claus in the middle of one night. It is no use praying for a gift of healing to be sent.

Each one of us is born with many potentialities, many

latent gifts. The challenges that come to us and the responses we make to them will largely determine which gifts will grow and develop and which will diminish. Some will be called upon and exercised while others will remain dormant or die away.

A few, of course, have found a gift of healing at a remarkably early age. Mr. Hickson discovered his vocation when he was only fourteen.

"We were sitting together one evening in the drawing room," he once related, "and a little cousin was suffering acutely from neuralgia; and in a simple way I was asking our Lord to help her when it suddenly came into my mind, almost as though the words had been spoken, 'Lay your hands on her face.' I did so, with the result that the pain vanished. . . . After this I had many cures and my mother told me that God was evidently working through me in healing the sick and that we must pray about it, asking Him to guide me in the right exercise of this ministry."

While some have been specially destined by God for a particular vocation, the gift of healing mostly develops from small beginnings. If you have a natural gift of understanding and sympathy, can share imaginatively in another's sufferings, and are moved with compassion, you have healing potentialities. If you feel drawn in this direction there are three things that ought to be done.

The first is to be a regular communicant. If you are to align yourself with Christ against the powers of evil you will need all the protection which He brings through the blessed sacrament. It is in this service that we realise the depth of what suffering means and Christ's victory in the midst of it and over it.

The second is to ask your vicar or minister about joining a prayer group. Here you will find yourself taking part in this ministry, not as an isolated unit, but as a member of Christ's Church. You will also need the help and discipline of prayer, for without prayer there is no healing. If a prayer group does not exist, ask if you can start one.

The third is to leave all planning to the guidance of the Holy Spirit. Sometimes, when a person feels he is called to heal he thinks something ought to be planned and that he ought to have a list of sick people to minister to. He will soon learn that planning is more hindrance than help to the working of the Holy Spirit.

We plan far too much and are always devising schemes for the advancement of the kingdom, and then asking God to bless them. We need more waiting upon God, more prayer groups, more awareness of what His guidance is. If we are really abiding in Him, then we do what comes naturally to us.

It is when we completely abandon our natural gifts to God, without self-interest, that they become transformed into gifts of the Holy Spirit. Then a new and mysterious actor enters. Confronted with a sick person, the Holy Spirit takes possession and we ourselves lose all personal desire to heal—sometimes even to a point of reluctance. We know what St. Paul meant when he said that he wanted to be nothing more than a slave in Christ's hands.

As we go on in simple obedience to the Holy Spirit, He guides us into situations where He wants to use us. How we respond will determine how or when the next occasion comes. We do not have to seek it. The Lord will "send" the occasions to us, and unexpected things will begin to happen.

Many who are called to this ministry at times experience a tingling in hands and fore-arms immediately before being impelled to lay on hands. This sensation is also felt during deep prayer and sometimes when in the company of people, one of whom may later ask for special help.

A new and "other" sensitivity may be the ability to locate by intuition and by touch the areas of a sufferer's body where trouble lies. Sometimes the ministrant's finger-tips feel heat or, alternatively, a "deadness" coming from those parts that need healing. Thus a healer knows instinctively how long he should hold his hands over the affected part. Sometimes his hands vibrate with the creative energies of God flowing through them. Later, the sufferer may say that he felt a "glow of warmth" or something like an electric current passing through him. Such events are not important in themselves—they are the outward manifestations of the working of the real Power within—though when they first come they can be highly disturbing.

The ministrant feels that he is being carried forward by this Power into a strange and wonderful world which cannot be adequately defined. At times he will feel frightened and insecure because he does not know what God is doing with him. He discovers also that he himself is becoming more vulnerable to the hurts of life and to the pressures of the evil one. All he can do then is to abandon himself more and more to the protection of Christ and the tender mercies of God.

He knows that the gift is not his and that it can be taken away. As long as God can use him the gift is given for the good of the whole body of Christ. "According as each hath received a gift, minister it among yourselves, as good stewards of the manifold grace of God" (1 Peter 4: 10).

Even then, it is not the gift that heals; but the power of the risen Christ, Who is not dependent for His mighty working on someone who happens to have the gift. The prayer of faith shall heal the sick! Even though our faith be only as a grain of mustard seed, He will use it when offered in complete sincerity and trust.

When as Christian believers we are confronted by any situation of need and we call upon the Holy Spirit for divine aid, He will supply whatever gifts are needed to resolve that situation. All He looks for is a trusting and receptive heart. He may supply not one gift but many. Thus, in one situation, in addition to the gifts of healing, He may also supply the gifts of faith, discernment and knowledge. To one who has abandoned himself to Christ and has been born of the Spirit, He provides all that is necessary for His working. As the father in the story of the prodigal son said, "Son, thou art ever with me and all that I have is thine."

The gift of healing cannot be switched on at will. The most that can be said of a healer is that he has become an instrument for God's use, a channel of the Holy Spirit for the incoming of His healing grace and mercies. And these are for the extension of Christ's kingdom into the life of our fallen world.

V

WE ALL NEED HEALING

NONE OF US can say that he is perfectly whole and has no need of our Lord's healing grace. You cannot divide the whole from the sick as you can the sheep from the goats. There may be moments when we attain that sublimely perfect poise with God and our fellows and with all creation which spells wholeness; but life is not static. It moves on and very soon we are caught up in all its imperfections again.

For we live in a "fallen" order and, whether we like it or not, we are involved with each other in "the sin of the world". We have our successes and failures, our joys and sorrows, our laughter and tears, and it is not always easy to keep on an even keel. We all are conscious of so many stresses and strains, and as life speeds up and the world grows smaller they press on us all the more. Sometimes we hurt each other when we least intend to and sometimes we get hurt by people or by circumstances through no fault of our own.

The build-up of these hurts over the years affects us deeply. They shape and mould us in every part of our being. Many of our illnesses are but precipitations in the physical region of our beings of what were originally spiritual or emotional hurts.

41

Some of them go back to our childhood days and are now seemingly "forgotten". We were unable to assimilate them harmoniously, at the time they happened, into our total experience. Others are more recent and we are still in the process of making adjustments to them. Some of the hurts that come our way go so deep that we cannot deal with them alone and we need the help of a friend who will share our burden.

What matters is not so much the hurts themselves as the response we bring to them. I do not use the word "react", for that belongs to the machine. A machine has no choice in the matter. If one button is pressed it will react in one way and if another is pressed it will react in yet another. But a human being has a choice in the response he makes. However much that choice might have become diminished by the manner of his previous responses he never loses it entirely.

Generally speaking, the response a person makes to the hurts of life may be either positive or negative. He can meet them positively by accepting and assimilating them into his total experience of life, or he can make the negative response of trying to refuse and reject them. If he rejects them he is allowing the primitive impulses that lie deep within each one of us to have complete sway over him either by his fighting the situation or by running away from it; or he will adopt the chameleon-like attitude of complete resignation.

Many ills originate in one or another of these negative responses. In this sense, therefore, what we so often call an illness is in fact the ultimate set of symptoms of a state of dis-ease that we may have been carrying for a long time. The negative response has finally precipitated itself into our physical body. There is often no sense, therefore, in praying that a sick person might recover his "former" health in which lay the seeds of his trouble.

There is the negative response of resentment, which is compounded of two basic emotions: the anger of the primitive creature within us wanting to fight and kill the enemy that is destroying our peace, and also the frustration that comes from having to conform to what society or Christian conscience tells us we must or must not do. A sudden resentment so strong that we become "consumed" by it, or a resentment which we cherish in our hearts over the years, is bound to have its effect on the body's chemistry and will ultimately affect the health of the whole person.

Fear is another negative response that can poison. I have known people whose lives have been crippled by fear. Sometimes it is a fear of the future—"what will happen if . . . ?" Sometimes it is a fear of the past, like a ghost waiting to assert itself again when least expected; or it is just a nameless fear that keeps the sufferer awake at night, afraid even of losing consciousness in sleep.

Grief, too, can be a killer. It is natural and right—and indeed healing—to experience a period of mourning when a loved one dies, but if we bottle it up or dwell too long within it our response can also become negative, and therefore harmful and destructive.

Making negative responses to the hurts we experience in life is common to all. They are part and parcel of our human inheritance. Deep within everyone are the primitive feelings of the brute creation. From the moment of our conception, each one of us recapitulates the whole process of the evolutionary system.

These negative responses are even more threatening to our well-being when positively encouraged and stirred up.

The words from the Litany come to mind here—"from envy, hatred and malice, and all uncharitableness, Good Lord, deliver us." We all know what these vices are, and to give way to any of them—even more, to stir them up within us—is to allow the metabolism of our whole being to become poisoned.

Jesus knew all about this "fallen" life with all its imperfections. He shared it with us. He came right into the midst of it. He became incarnate in it. In becoming man He shared with us the brute instincts and primitive reflexes that are written into our natures.

If anyone was hurt, He was. His message was rejected, He was betrayed by one of His own disciples, denied by another and deserted by them all, but He never complained, "Why should this happen to me?" He never allowed resentment to hold any sway over Him. He was condemned, tortured, crucified, yet He never let His mind fill with fear.

He accepted it all. He absorbed and assimilated all the hurts that came His way and His response to them was continually positive. Even as they took their hammers and drove in the nails, He accepted it all and still gave back Love. "Father," He said, "forgive . . ."

In all things He was the victor. He conquered life. Of Satan and his kingdom of evil, Jesus could truly say, "He hath nothing in Me."

This is the positive way, the victorious way we all eventually have to learn. It is the only way to life and health. We are healed only when we are prepared to change direction. But we cannot find this way by ourselves. It can be found only in Him Who is the Way, the Truth and the Life.

Sometimes we talk about people being expert in one

field or another—in music, mathematics, cooking or in sport. But of whom can it be said that he or she is expert in living life victoriously and in meeting all that comes, of good and ill, "with gallant and high-hearted happiness, giving thanks for all things"? Only of the Christ. He alone knows and shows the way.

Though He knew this "fallen" life and shared it with us, He also knew that other life, that perfect life as His Father originally made it and ultimately intends it to be. He could see this perfect life so clearly as He moved about among us. He saw it in the leper who came to Him asking to be healed, He saw it in Joanna while her face was still largely hidden by her shawl. He sees it in every one. He sees a world released from the powers of evil, a world that has found its divinely-purposed perfection by becoming the kingdom of God.

The greatest prayer in the world is the one He gave us. I do not think anyone can realise anything like the full implications of it. Yet He could see what it meant were it to be fully realised. "Thy kingdom come, Thy will be done, on earth as it is (in this moment) in heaven."

Every healing work of our Lord was a sign, a showing forth of His kingdom, a manifestation of God's perfect will done on earth as it is in heaven. It was a proclamation of the good news, of His victory over Satan. Every time He healed a sick man something of cosmic significance was happening. He was undoing the consequences of the "fall". He was restoring man's lost image. He was bringing immortality to light.

He proclaims the good news of His kingdom as much in His healing works as in His preaching and teaching.

In a sense, then, what Jesus showed us was that we have two lives. First, this earthly life of which we are so conscious, the life we are now living here in this imperfect world where sin and sickness abound and we are as captives. Secondly, there is that other life which Jesus could so clearly see, a perfect life which exists even now in the Mind of God, not in some vague distant future. It is this other life, this perfect life, that the Christ has come to bring. By His victory over all the powers of evil He makes it possible for God's perfection to be released in us. He does this through His forgiving and His cleansing and His healing power.

I sometimes think of God as the great Sculptor who is sculpturing out of us that perfection which He has for each one of us and, indeed, for all creation. We sometimes talk of the good and the bad experiences that come our way, but I am convinced that when we reach that final perfection that is God's perfect will for us, we shall look back and say, "No, they weren't good experiences and bad experiences. Every one was needful, and therefore potentially all were good." The great Sculptor needed every one of them.

What we did not realise was that it was not the experiences that really mattered but the kind of responses we brought to them. If we responded positively by accepting and absorbing them we were co-operating with Him, but if our response was negative, bitter, hostile, resentful, we were refusing to let His perfect will be done in us and therefore were standing in the way of our own good health.

VI

THE HEALING TOUCH

JESUS WAS THE PERFECT Channel of God's power to release and heal, and this is what He wants His body, the Church, to be. With every part of His being He communicated to us the fruit of His victory over this fallen world. Sometimes we sing one of our favourite hymns:

Fill Thou my life, O Lord my God,
In every part with praise,
That my whole being may proclaim
Thy Being and Thy ways.

Not for the lip of praise alone
Nor e'en the praising heart,
I ask, but for a life made up
Of praise in every part.

Fill every part of me with praise,
Let my whole being speak
Of Thee and of Thy love, O Lord,
Poor though I be and weak.

Every part of me! Our Lord conveys the transforming power of His gospel not only through His lips as He preaches, but also through the touch of His hand.

If there were any truth in the statement I heard long ago—that the purpose of His healing work was to draw attention to His preaching and teaching, I should want to counter it by saying that much of His preaching and teaching is a spoken commentary on His healing work. The truth, of course, lies somewhere between the two.

He communicates His kingdom to us through His lips as He preaches but He conveys it also, with equal power, through the touch of His hands.

Even on our ordinary human level there are times, indeed, when words fail and only the touch of a hand can convey what is in one's heart. Have you ever sat at the bedside of a friend who is desperately ill and struggled hard to find the right words to speak? However hard you tried you somehow felt that words could never really convey all that you wanted to convey. The phrases that came to you would have sounded pious and empty. The only thing you were able to do was to hold the hand of your friend.

As you sat there you knew that your friend had been helped. You felt something of his suffering enter into your own being. His burden had been shared.

Or perhaps a neighbour, having suddenly heard some tragic news, came bursting into your house and all you were able to do was to put your arm about him.

Jesus used the simple touch. There was nothing "magical" in this. I often wish we could find a phrase other than "the laying-on-of-hands" for all it really means is "the touch of Christ", Who in His compassion and power shares and heals.

The touch of Christ—or the laying-on-of-hands given in His name—does two things. First, it conveys His sharing in the sufferings of our common humanity.

48

Secondly, it conveys His divine authority over all the powers of evil that afflict us.

First, His sharing with us in our human sufferings. This, surely, is what must have been felt by the leper who was "untouchable" and an outcast. No one would go near him because of his sickness. He was made to live apart in a world of his own.

It is said that St. Francis of Assisi, a later disciple of our Lord, came across such a sufferer when walking with some of his followers. They wanted to avoid him but St. Francis ran to the man, threw his arm around him and kissed him. "This," he said, "is what my Lord would have done."

I am sure that long afterwards when the leper recounted the story of his healing he would remember most of all that "He touched me!"

This touch of Jesus was felt by many who came to Him to be healed. The woman who pressed through the crowd just to touch the hem of His garment felt His power of healing love fill her whole body. To touch Him, or to be touched by Him, was what sufferers needed then and still need now. For here was One who, though different from all other men, was yet one of themselves, a Man Who understood.

Time and again we read that He was moved with compassion. The word has lost some of its meaning nowadays and, with it, the Greek word "sympathy" too. So, to try to describe this deep, inward movement of sharing in another's sufferings we are using the word "empathy" instead. This inward movement, healing in itself, was conveyed to the sufferer by His touch. He shared, He knew, He understood. He came to the sufferer just where he was.

I remember a patient in the psychiatric hospital where I had the privilege of being resident chaplain for some four years. He had been a Greek patriot captured by the Nazis. They tried to get him to talk but he wouldn't, so they tortured him. As he persisted in his silence they took his little family and shot them one by one. Finally, they cut off the tip of his tongue and threw him into prison. Mercifully, his friends managed to rescue him and he was brought to our hospital in England.

The psychiatrists did all they could for him but their most difficult problem was that every time he began to become normal the memory of what had happened to his family would drive him back once again into his dark and unreal world. He just did not want to get well.

We called him Napoleon and I eventually got to know him well, though it was difficult at first to hold much conversation with him because of the impediment in his speech.

One day I said, "Napoleon, it may be very difficult to find anyone who really understands what you have been through and how you feel now, but I think I know One Who can. Why not join us in our chapel services on Sunday?"

He was delighted to be asked as he had thought that being a member of the Greek Orthodox Church he might not be welcomed. I reassured him and said that the chapel was open to all. I think he then began to realise that not everyone in the world was against him.

The chapel, a pleasant enough Victorian building, could hold two or three hundred patients. Every Sunday some found their own way from the wards and others were escorted by nurses; and most of the pews were full. I still have a sense of wonder as I remember the poor condition of some of the patients, for as soon as they had passed through the doors they became quiet and still. Never have I heard hymns sung with such sincerity and fervour as in that place. The "amens" were glad and joyful affirmations of the prayers that were offered.

Sometimes, as they knelt at the rails to receive Holy Communion, they would look up and thank me as though I were giving them the most precious diamond in the world. But they knew that the little fragment of bread was worth far, far more than that!

Napoleon had one or two habits foreign to our Anglican ways but which seemed to mean much to him. These he brought with him from his own Church. Always, before entering the chapel, he wanted to kiss my hand and, during the prayers, he wanted to stand rather than kneel. We arranged that he should occupy the back pew.

I don't know how or when it began, but after a few weeks I realised that Napoleon was leaving his dark and unreal world behind. It was obvious that something was happening to him during those chapel services. There was an intenseness about him that was almost tangible. It may have been the fervour of the singing, or something he was appreciating in the Bible readings or the sermons or the prayers, or a combination of them all.

But I have a feeling that more than anything else it was the carved alabaster figure of the Christ upon His cross that stands over and behind the altar. I don't like many of these Victorian carvings, but this one is particularly good. I often saw him gazing at it.

He was finding Someone who really did understand, Someone Who had entered as deeply into the world of suffering as he had done, and gone even deeper. Many had offered pity and sympathy and had done all that they could for him, but here he was finding One with

51

that deep empathy that really understood and shared. As he received the laying-on-of-hands it was to him the touch of the Master Who once was crucified, the touch that reached right down to just where he was.

It was about four months after the day that he first began to come to our chapel services that his psychiatrist and I stood on the steps at the front door to wave him goodbye. The psychiatrist, a Roman Catholic exiled from his native Poland, told me that he knew Who it was Who had brought healing to his patient.

Secondly our Lord's touch conveys His divine authority. It was this authority that the evil spirits were quick to recognise: "We know Thee who Thou art; the Holy One of God!"

The centurion seeking Jesus' help for his servant knew it: "I am not worthy that Thou shouldst come under my roof . . . speak the word only and my servant shall be healed. For I also am a man set under authority, having under myself soldiers, and I say to this one 'Go' and he goeth . . . and to my servant 'Do this' and he doeth it."

It was this divine authority that Jesus called upon when, at the bedside of Simon Peter's mother-in-law, He rebuked the fever. It was this same authority He invoked as He cast out evil spirits from demented minds.

The authority of Jesus was, and is, unlike any other that the world has ever seen. The common folk were astonished by it, the disciples amazed by it, the religious leaders jealous of it, and the zealots, their minds filled with thoughts of release from their Roman oppressors, were confused by it.

It was the authority of the kingdom of God's perfection and it had power to set people free from bondage.

Jesus delegated this authority to His disciples. In what I believe He intended to be a training mission for the future Church He sent them forth two by two and "gave them power and authority over all devils and to cure diseases. He sent them forth to preach the kingdom and to heal the sick." And then, later, after His ascension, "they went forth and preached everywhere, the Lord working with them and confirming the word with signs following."

He never withdrew this authority and He never gave the slightest hint that it would ever be withdrawn or in any way become lessened.

Certainly, in the early days of the Church, preaching the kingdom and healing the sick went unhesitatingly hand in hand. This divine authority was the only kind of authority the infant Church knew. Not for them were palaces and cathedrals and all the outward paraphernalia of what sometimes might appear as signs of worldly authority. These were the days before the Church became official. Constantine's conversion was yet to come.

Then came a fundamental change in the Church's thinking about illness. The thousands upon thousands of pagans who were being baptised into the Christian Church brought their thinking habits with them. The Graeco-Roman philosophies in which they had been brought up for many a generation had regarded sickness not as an enemy invader but as God-sent! Either it was a punishment for sin or a testing-time for the soul's good. We have never really rid ourselves of these parasitic ideas.

They have been responsible ever since for the Church so largely neglecting her healing ministry. How can a clergyman minister to the sick for healing if part of his mind thinks that God allows sickness for a special purpose? And how can we blame a relative of a sick person saying, "Oh well! It is God's will"?

The authority which Jesus gives to His Church has to be accepted fully if it is to have any purposeful meaning at all.

I believe that when the whole Church—the whole body of Christ—recovers her faith in Christ's authority over sickness and sin we shall see many more wonderful healing works. The few that we are seeing today are indications of what could happen when His promises are fully claimed again.

VII

UNDER DIVINE AUTHORITY

THE ORDAINED MAN, priest or minister, has no choice whether or not he should exercise the ministry of healing. He is a man under authority, called apart by God to accept and fulfil His Lord's two-fold commission. He may feel that he has no special gift in that direction but he must nevertheless allow himself to be used by our Lord as an instrument in His hands. Some clergy may feel that they have no special gift for preaching but that does not prevent them from going into the pulpit every Sunday!

But the exercise of the healing ministry through the laying-on-of-hands is not confined to the clergy. The ascension-tide commission of our Lord vests authority in the believer, ordained or lay. "*He that believes* shall lay hands on the sick and they shall recover."

If a Christian believes that He "is the same, yesterday, today and forever", and that the power of his Lord to heal broken lives and to transform human situations has not lessened, and further that his life is no longer his own but belongs to the Lord Who can use him, he can be a channel of divine grace. He may not know why or how or when the Lord might want to use him, but if he is continually aware of His Lord's shaping and guiding, he may sometimes feel a strong inward movement of the Spirit urging him to lay hands on a sufferer.

Remembering that this act is in essence simply the touch of Jesus, we need not envisage it as being something very formal. He does not have suddenly to announce that he will give the sufferer the laying-on-of-hands. The very fact that he is there, sharing with his friend, may be sufficient healing in itself to warrant nothing more. But when he does feel a compelling urge, which he knows is born of the Spirit, to communicate the healing love and compassion of Christ through his human touch, it may be that just to take his friend's hands in his own is all that is necessary. What matters at this point is his inward prayer of the heart that through this touch Christ's healing power will flow into the soul and mind and body of his friend.

Another method is simply to suggest to his friend that they might join in a short time of prayer together. He need not say anything more than that, but at some time during the prayer he can put his hands on the sufferer's head and pray that they might become a channel of our Lord's healing grace.

It is important that such an act should be quite natural and that, as far as possible, it should flow out of the conversation that has preceded it. The laying-on-of-hands should be given quietly and without fuss; this is the Christ-like way.

I shall later have more to say about this and about the need of faith, but we will now concern ourselves with Holy Unction (or "Anointing with oil"). The New

Testament vests the authority for giving Holy Unction in the clergy. "Is any among you sick, let him call for the elders of the Church . . ."

There is no doubt that, as I have already suggested, a special authority is vested in the man who is ordained, and I should like to say something about this before looking at the sacrament itself.

I shall always be deeply thankful to the saintly old priest who spoke to me about this matter when I was a young curate. We had been to a meeting in his parish at which I had been asked to give the address and I had given him a lift home in my car. Before getting out of the car he put his hand on my knee and said, "Just one thing I would like to say to you, George; accept your priestly authority. You haven't done so yet. It will make your ministry complete." Coming from such a man, I felt very moved. His wise, kindly advice has helped me through the years and, I pray, has been a help to me in trying to help others.

When a clergyman has humbly accepted this God-given authority and made it his own, it somehow affects all his ministry and it communicates itself to those who come to him for help.

Until that time, for example, I had been reticent about what we call the sacrament of penance—sacramental confession and absolution—feeling so strongly that only One could forgive! But through the years I have learned its power.

No one is under compulsion to use it. There are some who ought to use it and many others who need it at least once in a while. The Book of Common Prayer is very wise about this. One of the Exhortations in the Holy Communion Service says: "If there be any of you who . . .

cannot quieten his own conscience but requireth further comfort or counsel, let him come to me or to some other discreet and learned Minister of God's Word and open his grief; that by the ministry of God's holy Word he may receive the benefit of absolution together with ghostly (i.e. spiritual) counsel and advice, to the quieting of his conscience and avoiding of all scruple and doubt-fulness."

I have had the wonderful and moving privilege of listening to the confessions of many people as they have opened their hearts to God, and of voicing in His name, and by that authority which is given to the ordained man, the divine forgiveness, cleansing and absolution. And every time I have felt the incoming power of God bringing release.

When I was warden of the Crowhurst Home of Healing there came to stay with us an old lady from Bavaria. Her name was well-known in Germany as a composer and translator. She had been advised by two old Munich friends to visit us, and the purpose of her visit, she said, was simply to enjoy three weeks' quiet holiday and rest in England.

She joined in the daily services in the chapel but when the day of our mid-week Holy Communion came she did not come to the rails to receive. Later, I discovered that she was a Roman Catholic. I told her that as long as people were staying in the Home there was no barrier as far as we were concerned. If she were a communicant in her own Church she was welcome to come to our Anglican services.

This little conversation led, in a wonderful way, to many things. She has since gone on into the fuller life, so I feel free to tell her story.

The first thing that happened was that she said she would like to accept the invitation but before doing so must make her confession. She indicated that there were many complications in her life. I offered to act as her confessor.

For a whole hour late one Saturday evening she poured out all her troubles. I soon began to realise that the real purpose of her visit was far more important to her than simply to enjoy a quiet holiday. Things had gone wrong in her life over thirty years before and ever since then she had felt ostracised from her Church, and therefore cut off from God. The fact that she had been unable to attend her "Mass" had been a terrible blow to her.

Tears were shed that night but they were tears of release and rejoicing. As I left her kneeling in the chapel it seemed that she was enveloped in a tremendous sense of peace.

She was one of the first to arrive for our Holy Communion service next morning. Her eyes were shining with a great happiness. The burden of the years had fallen away.

It was not until her three weeks' stay was over and she had returned home that I discovered the real reason for her visit. She had been suffering from cancer and had been told by her doctors that she had about three months to live.

But I know that after she had been with us only a few days this reason had given way to something far more important. She forgot her illness in a newly-found desire to be at peace once more with God and His Church. One of her doctor friends wrote to tell me that the cancer had been arrested but what had impressed him more profoundly still was the complete change in her personality. She was alive with happiness now.

Some two years later she arranged for me to go to Germany to discuss the current revival of the Church's healing ministry with an abbot in close touch with Rome. He was very happy that the sacrament of Holy Unction had been restored as a healing sacrament in the Roman Church and was immensely interested in what was happening in the healing ministry throughout the Anglican communion. So she played her part in the forward movement of the healing ministry and also in the ecumenical movement! Before she died, she had been fully restored to her own Church.

God has wonderfully given a sacramental life to His Church, and both the sacrament of penance and that of Holy Unction play an important part in it as far as the Church's ministry of healing is concerned.

What happens in a sacrament is that our Lord takes a natural thing and invests it with the supernatural. Thus, in Holy Communion He takes bread, the natural food, and when it is consecrated He uses it to convey to us the supernatural food from heaven—His very Self. Again, in Baptism, He takes water, the natural cleansing agent, and when it is blessed He uses it to convey the supernatural washing away of our past so that we become born anew into the family of Christ's Church.

Similarly, in Holy Unction, olive oil, the natural healing emollient, is used. In our Lord's parable of the Good Samaritan wine is used to disinfect the traveller's wounds and oil to bring healing. Oil, with its natural penetrative qualities, is still used today as a base for other medicaments. So we set it apart for God's use in consecration that it may convey to us also the supernatural power of God to heal.

Let us turn again to the New Testament to see what the elders are called to do and what the consequences of Holy Unction are. "Let them pray over him, anointing him with oil in the name of the Lord. And the prayer of faith shall save him that is sick, and the Lord shall raise him up; and if he has committed sins, it shall be forgiven him."

While it is primarily a sacrament of healing it also contains within itself a forgiveness of sins. In other words, the absolution is not separate; it is incidental to, and a vital part of, the total healing ministration given. It speaks of wholeness and it is addressed to the heart and soul of the sufferer as well as to his mental and physical distress.

But while it is a sacrament of healing there is more to it than this. Holy Unction is a consecrating sacrament. It is used to set apart a person as a vessel of God's grace.

I once thought that the only difference between the laying-on-of-hands and Holy Unction lay in the difference of authority—ordained or lay—of those who happened to be ministering. But after having ministered to many hundreds of sick people I began to realise that there was much more to it than that.

Why was it, I began to wonder, that at the end of a personal interview when I sought guidance on what to do for the sufferer, the answer almost invariably seemed to be the laying-on-of-hands and only very infrequently Holy Unction? I tried, prayerfully, to find an understanding and I can only record the answer that seemed to be given. For myself, I have found it entirely satisfying. The answer seemed to be that Holy Unction was for the "deep" illnesses.

When a person becomes ill, his illness is usually recognisable as an entity separate from himself. He is a person carrying an illness. But in the case of a deep illness he is not so much a person with an illness; he is a *sick person*.

Sicknesses like cancer and disseminated sclerosis come immediately to mind. Though I still never take it as a foregone conclusion but rather prefer to wait on the guidance of the Holy Spirit on what form of ministration I should give to the sufferer (for we are concerned with persons more than with illnesses), I always prepare myself for Holy Unction on these occasions.

This is just a hunch, but I have an instinctive feeling that through the laying-on-of-hands the movement of healing power works from the outside and into a person, whereas in Holy Unction the healing, creative powers of God begin from within. It is like planting a seed in the heart of the soil or—more dramatically—like planting an atom bomb in the very core of the situation to separate the roots of the illness from the personality of the sufferer himself.

I used to be inwardly fearful when confronted by these deep illnesses. Since childhood we have been brought up in an atmosphere of "unfaith". We have been told that certain illnesses are incurable and that there is no hope. I thought of them as a kind of sound barrier through which nothing could penetrate and that in the ministry of healing we could go so far and no farther. But I have gone on in faith that with God nothing is impossible, and having ministered to such sufferers many times I can only witness to the fact that even these deep illnesses are not beyond the reach of our Lord's healing power.

Time and again, following Holy Unction, there has been a profound change in the sufferer's whole personality and outlook and the prognosis has gone all awry. Sometimes, indeed, the sickness has been arrested and at other times the expected three months left to live have become two years and more. In every case, as far as I remember, the sufferer has been lifted on to a new plane of life in which the damage that has been caused no longer hurts—physically as well as spiritually—as it did or as medically it would be expected to do. Furthermore, I have observed that a wondrous change, beyond the reckoning of human understanding, has taken place in the lives of the sufferers.

I remember how two nurses, unknown to each other and of about the same age, came to a service of healing. Both had cancer and had been ministered to. There was much rejoicing in the heart of one of them as she came up to the communion rails to receive the laying-on-of-hands in an act of surrender and thanksgiving, for her trouble had been completely arrested and she had been given an "all clear" by the doctors. The other was unable to get up the steps to the sanctuary so I ministered to her in the pew.

I also visited this nurse in her flat which she shared with another young woman. She said to me:

"This is the first time I've been on the receiving end of prayer and it is wonderful. I've joined in prayer with my friends for the healing of many people and I am now finding what it is like to be so blessed. I know you won't feel sorry for me because paradise seems so close and I would not have this realisation taken from me for anything that anyone could give. If only we could experience a thing like this when life is normal! What a difference it would make to the world!"

She died peacefully about three months later. She had been wonderfully uplifted above her suffering and for this I gave thanks.

VIII

CASTING OUT DEVILS

ONE CANNOT GO FAR in the healing ministry without being confronted by the need of yet another ministration—exorcism, or the casting out of evil.

In my early days in the ministry I had an open mind on whether or not there was a personal devil. I was then prepared to accept that all the word "Satan" meant was a personification of all evil. But this theological abstraction, culled mostly from the academic security of my theological college days, could not hold ground for long. In my ordinary pastoral ministry I was always coming face to face with situations and sicknesses which could not be explained away in ordinary human terms. It was not until I came to accept that Satan does indeed exist and that evil spirits can still wreck human lives that I was able to help, with any real power, certain of the sufferers I met. To put it only on a pragmatic level, exorcism worked!

It was about that time that I studied the gospels afresh. There was no doubt, in my mind, about the grim struggle that took place beneath the surface between Jesus and the "prince of this world". Though He knew more about psychology than any of us will ever know, He never explained evil away in what might now be called psychological terms. He met it face to face. Whenever He was confronted by the power of evil He overcame it for what it was—an enemy invader, a despoiler of His Father's creation.

Though a knowledge of psychology and of psychiatric practice may be a help to a Christian minister it is not vital. What is vital is that he has the "gift of discernment of spirits". It would be a rejection of his calling were he to try to be something other than he is. God calls a minister to be a minister of the gospel and a psychiatrist to be a psychiatrist.

As members of the Christian Church, ordained or lay, we are concerned not only with the sick and suffering but also with something even more fundamental—a spiritual warfare against all the forces of evil. "For our fight is not against human foes, but against cosmic powers, against the authorities and potentates of this dark world, against the superhuman forces of evil in the heavens" (Eph. 6: 12. N.E.B.).

In this larger field psychology is limited and has little to say. It is only from the spiritual aspect that we become aware, for example, of places where a climate of evil exists. There are occasions when an atmosphere of evil in a building or an area can be discerned.

I remember having had charge of a church which had been bombed during the war and had not been used for worship for some years. I felt deeply worried because I sensed evil in the place. It was something deeper than the evil of the bombing and I was not surprised when an old parishioner told me that sometimes late at night he had seen people going to the place and had heard them chanting strangely. He could not say that black magic was being practised but I could see he felt that it might have been.

I was anxious to move back into the church and to use it again for Christian worship; with the use of a huge tarpaulin for shelter, mid-week celebrations of the Holy Communion were begun. Only two or three people attended. My intention was that the Blessed Sacrament be so lifted up that, were any evil present, it would be completely driven out. Each week we moved to a different part of the church and I "knew" that light was driving out darkness.

I was grateful for the help of three friends in particular. One was a head-deaconess, a deeply spiritual woman who often visited the parish, another was Father Gilbert Shaw, a London priest well-known for his contribution to the Church's understanding in this field, and the third was my old friend, Godfrey Mowatt.

Though Godfrey was blind he could "see" much farther than the rest of us. He first came to that parish to conduct a service of healing in the church hall, where we held our Sunday services at that time. He knew nothing of the spiritual struggle that was going on but, at his own insistent request, I took him along to "see" the church. I can picture him now, standing just inside the door, a heap of shovels and a wheelbarrow at his side. His face fell and he muttered something, but I did not ask him what he had said. Some months later, when the building was re-opened for worship, he returned to conduct another service of healing. As I guided him through the door he suddenly halted, his face lit up, and he exclaimed, "How full of light it is!" After the service I asked him if he could remember his impressions on his first visit.

"Oh, how very dark the church was then!" he said. "But there's a great light there now."

Missionaries from abroad have found that in some areas the feeling of evil is so oppressive that they have had to draw on all the resources of spiritual energy available to overcome it—an experience that was common to the missionary saints of old. St. Patrick had it in Ireland and composed his hymn "The Deer's Cry" from which our "St. Patrick's Breastplate" has been evolved, as a divine protection against the idolatry and witchcraft then existing in that country. In the central part of this hymn he made a three-fold sign of the Cross, like an invisible shield, about him:

> "Christ with me, Christ before me, Christ behind me;
> Christ in me, Christ below me, Christ above me;
> Christ at my right, Christ at my left;
> Christ in breadth, in length, in height."

Society does not generally realise how much it owes to the spread of Christianity. Once a country's life has become permeated by the faith which we all so easily take for granted, that country becomes healthy, prosperous and happy. But now we live in days of change, and one dreads to contemplate what might be the eventual results if our permissive society gains ground. Today's boy or girl dying from heroin or senselessly committing damage, injury or worse while under the influence of any mind-bending drug is an inevitable consequence of the evil let loose by the abandonment of the Christian faith. I am not surprised when a friend of mine, much used in the exorcist ministry, says that there has been a big increase in the cases of devil possession in the last few years.

The atmosphere, or spiritual climate, in which we live affects our well-being as much as does the food we eat and the air we breathe. Animals and even plants are not un-affected by it. When visiting a sick parishioner I have sometimes sensed an atmosphere of such evil that the sufferer has had little chance of getting better.

A young father once asked me to minister to his little boy. The child had no particular long-standing illness but was always suffering from one ailment or another. The father, near to a nervous breakdown though he did not mention it at the time, did not indicate what the source of the boy's trouble might be. It did not take me long to find out. When I got to the house it was like walking into a black cloud. I sensed the evil as soon as I entered the front door. It was not until several minutes later that his wife came in. I have never felt a more bitter hatred than that which flowed from her. What had caused this in the first place I do not know. But she had allowed this evil to happen to her; and it had become an open doorway for the dark powers to enter that home. I kept in touch with that little family. The father and his son are very happy now. His wife died later from a severe illness of the nervous system.

Not all who come under the power of the evil one do so as a result of their surrounding climate. Rather, they have themselves as individuals become affected. As in the fore-going case they have become so obsessed by a bitterness of spirit that the control of their free-will has been abandoned to it. They have become so overcome with self-pity follow-ing shock or grief that in the unbalanced mental and spiritual state which follows they can see only what is bad. The doors of their souls have been opened to the spirit of evil. It is also possible they have dabbled

69

in the occult, thereby inviting evil entities into their lives.

Before such sufferers are given Holy Unction or the laying-on-of-hands the invading spirit of evil must first be driven out. Thanks be to God, the power of the risen Christ has as much power today as ever it had of old. Whether or not the sufferer knows this, the evil entity present certainly does! It is amazing how effective the old phrases are when spoken with unhesitating authority: "In the name of Jesus of Nazareth I command you to come out." "In the name of Jesus, Son of the most high God, I command you . . ." And the old evangelical phrase, "By the power of His blood shed on Calvary . . ." is also full of power.

The ministry of exorcism covers three main areas. The first is concerned with rebuking; the second with the driving out of an obsessive spirit of evil pervading the sufferer's life; and, finally, with the exorcising of a possessing evil entity.

Rebuking is born of a Christ-desire to see the sufferer liberated from whatever illness binds him. It springs from a desire in the heart of the Christian helper when confronted by a destroying power. Jesus Christ condoned sickness no more than He condoned sin. Taken to see Simon's wife's mother, He *rebuked* the fever. He did not simply put soothing hands on her brow or offer words of comfort. He recognised it as an enemy invader and dealt with it as such.

Sometimes I have been led by the Spirit to rebuke a sufferer's illness and I have often wondered why. One reason may have been that the rebuking helped the sufferer to realise that his or her illness was not sent by God. There is also the possibility that, in some deep and mysterious way, infecting colonies of viruses, where they exist, have some sort of consciousness and are accordingly affected by a rebuke in Christ's Name.

Exorcism of an Obsessive Spirit is concerned with the driving out of an evil that is present in the sufferer's life, such as depression, hatred and other destroying emotions.

Soon after I became warden of the Home of Healing at Crowhurst I met a woman who was suffering from deep depression. At this time I had just come from being resident chaplain of one of our leading psychiatric hospitals. At first I thought she needed the benefit of psychiatric treatment but before I could voice this thought there came to me an inner challenging voice: "I did not bring you here to be an amateur psychiatrist but to minister the power of My Healing Grace."

Heeding the promptings of this inner voice I took her into the little chapel where in the Name of Christ I firmly rebuked the spirit of darkness that was destroying her life, and commanded it to go. Later that day I could hardly recognise her for she was a happy and changed woman.

Fear and many other negative emotions frequently control their victims who are obsessed by them. It is useless to tell such sufferers to pull themselves together. They need a friend's help, preferably that of a Christian minister, to achieve for them what they are unable to do for themselves.

There was one woman who could not walk a step without the aid of a friend supporting her. Even a walking stick was of no help. A friend brought her by car to see me and we spent some time together as she told me her story.

She knew it was "silly" but to me it was a diabolical thing that had happened to her. I could *feel* the evil that had her in its grip. In the holy name of Jesus I commanded it—three times, as is usual—to come out of her. She collapsed in her chair. After a few moments I put my hands on her head and prayed that the Holy Spirit would fill her soul, mind and body.

A little later we walked in the garden. For the first few steps she held on to my arm, but soon she felt confident enough to take her own weight. I remember her steps; they were long strides as though she was having to learn to walk all over again. Each step was deliberately made. She had difficulty managing the corners and in turning round to retrace her steps, but in a little while she could walk by herself. As she left I gave her a text to hold on to: "I can do all things in him who strengthens me" (Phil. 4: 13).

About a week later she wrote me a very happy letter. She had been out shopping by herself for the first time in many years. Her shopping finished, she had found a church in the High Street and had gone in to give thanks.

Finally comes the *Exorcising of a Possessing Evil Entity*.

A young woman who had suffered from mental and physical illnesses did not want to see me but had been brought by a friend. Her first words were, "You can't help me. Nobody can! I sold myself to the devil two years ago." I asked her to tell me about it. She complained that there had been trouble all through her life. She had been an unwanted child in the first place. Then had come a harsh blow. A love-affair had gone wrong and had made her very bitter against God. It was then she had decided to give herself to the devil.

Mercifully, she gained confidence as she told me her story and I was able to minister to her. She swayed as I did so, as if she were about to faint, and then suddenly collapsed. I helped her to a chair and laid my hands on her, praying the Holy Spirit to flood her whole being with His light and love. In a few moments I was able to leave, for she remained sitting, perfectly relaxed.

After about half-an-hour she got up and walked about like someone in a dream. Two or three days later she asked me what had happened as she could not remember much of our conversation or the ministration. She only knew that something evil had passed away and that life was now extremely good; she became a regular member of her church and was soon preparing for confirmation.

It is strange how such sufferers only vaguely remember the exorcism itself. All they know is that they have emerged out of a dark night into the sunlight.

Whether we use the rebuking of an illness or the driving out of an obsessive spirit of evil pervading the sufferer's life or the exorcising of a possessing evil entity, we identify ourselves with Christ's own ministry of compassion for those who suffer. Behind each of these aspects of the ministry of exorcism is His wondrous love of the individual and His desire to see his release from the things that hurt and bind him.

Psychiatry, too, has its part to play, but it cannot provide that new vision of what life can be when lived in His kingdom, nor the power to begin life afresh on a new plane. Only the divine love that springs from Christ's ministry of redemption can do that. Only in Christ can newness of life be found.

IX

PERSONAL INTERVIEWS

I wish that we could find a better word than counsel-
ling. It lacks that note of authority which the Lord lays
upon us when He commissions us to preach the Kingdom
and heal the sick; it often seems to suggest instead a picture
of two people discussing various ways to solve a problem.

Not that the minister, ordained or lay, is necessarily any
better than the sufferer who comes to him. Indeed, he
may be very conscious of need in his own life. But it is
wonderful how God uses him as a channel of healing even
when he is far from being at his best! I look back with a
deep sense of gratitude to those occasions when great
blessings have been brought to sufferers even when I have
personally been going through a very dark period.

The sufferer is seeking not a *man's* help, however experienced or dedicated the man may be; he is seeking God's
help. He may not admit it or be consciously aware of it;
but when he is sick or in trouble that is really what he is
looking for. The meeting with the minister may be the
climax of an experience that began long before, when the
Spirit of God first put it into the sufferer's mind to ask for
help. God was already at work in his situation and
brought him to the minister or lay friend that he might
find Him.

The depth of an interview with a sick person and the divine power that comes through to him in the ministration that follows are very largely decided by the degree of prayerful preparation given to it beforehand. The same truth applies to a public service of healing and to every service of the Church. I like very much the vestry prayers that take place in our Free Churches where minister and deacons meet for a time of quiet and expectant prayer before the public Service of Worship begins. Personally, I like to go apart for an hour before conducting a service of healing.

During the preparation no plan is made as to what is to be said to the sufferer or what form of ministration is to be given to him. One has to remember that he is a person quite different from any other. However much his illness or state of dis-ease may be similar to others, he must be dealt with as a unique person. God has something He wants to give to *him*. What this particular help will be He will reveal when the moment comes. If the time of preparation is used to be with Christ, to abide in His Spirit, what has to be said and what has to be done for the sufferer will be shown "in that hour".

For it is in the "now" that we find God. All healing flows from His creative energies actively at work in the world at any given moment. Often, when people talk about the creation, they give the impression that they think it all happened long ago, that at the beginning of time God created the universe in much the same way as a ship-builder builds a ship, that the moment came when He had completed His work and then bade it farewell to sail by itself across the oceans of time. But the truth is that *God has not finished His work*. The forces of His creative energies have never been withdrawn. They are all about

75

us in each passing moment and continuously at work within us.

Jesus said, "My Father worketh hitherto and I work." There is a sense of the timeless present about all of our Lord's work. There is never any hurry. It was said of Him that He is the Son of Man Who *is* in heaven—not "who came from heaven" or "who is going to heaven". In any given moment of time the full forces of the Father's creative and healing energies can flow through Him unhindered and unchecked. "I come," He said, "to do the works of Him that sent Me."

The Christian, therefore, prepares himself by dwelling in the Spirit of Christ, so that without hurry or any preconceptions he can put his heart, mind, voice and hands at God's disposal.

It is not only the sufferer who is coming to find God; it is the helper also. The interview is going to be a shared experience of God at work in the "now", and it will affect the helper as much as it does the sufferer.

There are four stages to an interview—the preparation, the conversation, the ministration and the after-care.

When I use the word "conversation" I think of this as being "two-way". On the one hand there is the conversation between sufferer and helper and, on the other, the continuing conversation between the ministrant and the risen Christ—or, if he prefers it, with the Holy Spirit. The helper is thus in a mid-way position, very much like that of an interpreter.

His conversation with the sufferer is of the nature of an I–Thou relationship, a conversation between two persons, one under authority and the other burdened, who are going to establish a bond; and this means that nothing is going to interrupt them for the next three-quarters of an hour or so. The ministrant is there not so much to give advice or to impose his own thoughts on what he would do in similar circumstances, but to listen—and at a deeper level than the spoken word. There begins to develop, beneath the words that are actually spoken, an unseen and unheard traffic of the soul.

The minister, outwardly relaxed but with a total awareness, is trying to find just where the sufferer is so that he can sit with him there. For this reason he keeps his own words to a minimum. The sufferer must completely unburden himself. As he begins to speak of his troubles the ministrant enters into the sufferer's own situation.

At first he will want to speak of his immediate or outward troubles—physical or mental—for these are what precipitated his desire to ask for help, but as the movement of the conversation develops and deepens he will, with a little prompting, begin to remember other things that have troubled him. And the helper, on his part, being concerned with the healing of the whole man, will encourage this.

Just before I sat down to write this chapter a man suffering from arthritis came to see me. Though he managed to drive his car he had great difficulty in getting up and down from a chair. He had been a keen bowls player and was a member of his county side until a few years ago when he had to give it up. He could not think of any special reason why his back should become so bad. He could not remember having knocked or twisted it. It came on gradually over the past few years.

He began to tell me about his home background, his work, his friends, and then I asked him, "You haven't had any time of worry or stress—before this began to happen?"

Suddenly he was silent. His eyes moistened and his voice shook.

"I lost my wife ten years ago," he said.

The silence hung in the air. It seemed to be a moment of truth. After a few moments, "Tell me," I said.

He told me. His wife had been perfectly well and happy. One evening she said she was tired and went to bed, leaving him to watch television. She was asleep when he followed her an hour later so he didn't disturb her. Early next morning he awoke to find that she was dead. . . .

After a little while I ministered to him.

Very often it is not what first prompts people to ask for help that matters most. It is something deeper, something that underlies the surface hurt. The real root of the trouble is within. Medical friends tell me that sometimes a patient will spend all his time asking help for some particular trouble and then, when the interview is over and the patient is leaving, he will turn back from the door and with a "By the way, doctor . . ." he will begin to indicate a deeper need.

It is into this deeper region that the ministrant is trying to penetrate—to share his suffering with him; and when the bond of sharing is established the ministrant begins to feel within himself the weight of the suffering. It is as though he is a mirror which reflects the sufferer's troubles. This sharing on a deep level, called "projective identification" by the psychotherapist, is a vital stage in the healing process.

To the Christian ministrant it will also be a sharing in the movement of his Lord's redemptive love. He will experience yet again the meaning of our Lord's incarnation as He shares with us all in our common humanity, and His sufferings upon the Cross when He bore all the sins of mankind. For no matter what the state of the sufferer might be, the ministrant knows that within himself are all the capacities which might have brought him, in similar circumstances, to the same point of disease. No longer are he and the sufferer two separate and distinct people. Joined together in an empathetic bond they can look together at the mess which evil has made of life.

The one saving feature of this situation is that the ministrant has never "let go" of that other conversation, the unseen conversation with the risen Christ. Any compassion he has felt has been the movement of Christ's compassion and any insights which have come to him have been born of the Spirit at work in him. It is wonderful how the Christ supplies His compassion and understanding for these interviews.

One reason for allowing the sufferer to unburden himself is that his problems are more easily exposed to the healing love of Christ in the ministration that follows.

When the sufferer has unburdened himself and the facts of his situation are, as much as possible, laid bare, there usually comes a long period of quiet. The ministrant uses this period to ask the risen Lord what it is He would have him say to the sufferer or do for him.

Is it the laying-on-of-hands or is it Holy Unction or is it some other form of ministration? The ministrant has available to him the words of the Bible (some apt text may have come to him which seems specially designed for this particular sufferer) and the whole range of the sacramental life of the Church (I use the word "sacramental" in its widest sense). Whatever it is he will accept and use it as a Christ-given channel of healing for this particular person. If it is Holy Unction he will probably say something like this: "I feel that I must give you Holy Unction but before doing so I want to explain what it means, so that you can say whether or not you would like to receive." I have never known anyone refuse. On the contrary, everyone to whom I have given this invitation has most gladly accepted it. It has seemed to be, from the sufferer's standpoint, just what he wanted.

If the ministration is something other than this, all that need be said at this point is that the first thing to be done is to take the whole matter to the Lord in prayer. The prayer preceding the ministration must surely be offered in Spirit-guided words, it must come out of that other, unseen conversation with the risen Christ, into which the burden is taken up. *A book of prayers simply will not do.* The prayer must convey in as few words as possible the whole burden of the sufferer and his failure to cope with it. And as the ministrant brings it all in prayer to our Lord he will feel a transference of the burden as it moves and finally comes to rest at the feet of Christ.

The inner disposition of the ministrant is tremendously important at the time of the ministration itself. His realisation of the surrounding presence of the divine Love will be unconsciously communicated to the sufferer. There must be no mental blockage in the channel! I mean by this that there must be no hesitant thoughts like "Will it damage the sufferer's faith if nothing happens?" or any conditional thoughts like "I hope he will come to church more often after this!" The ministrant must give himself unstintingly to the movement of God's creative activity at work in the "now". There must be a complete self-emptying of his own heart and mind.

After the ministration is over the ministrant and sufferer will experience a measure of exhaustion and it will be wise to leave the sufferer alone for a few minutes. Then, after a little while, it is helpful to suggest to him that he quietly spends the next hour by himself, abiding in the surrounding love of our Lord and giving thanks. This is the beginning of the after-care period.

The time of quiet and the giving of thanks are important. The first because the Lord has given a gift and there must now be time to assimilate it and make it his own. I used to wonder why Jesus often said, "Go home and tell no one." I think that part of the reason may have been that He knew the "world" well enough to know what it would try to do to the sufferer who was newly healed. People are so quick to say, "Oh! But that was just suggestion! The feeling will soon pass!" A healing ministration is something like the planting of a seed. It must be given time to establish itself. It is not easy at this stage for the erstwhile sufferer to say, "One thing I know!" That will come later.

The giving of thanks is important for two reasons as well as the obvious one that it is meet and right so to do. The first reason is that a thankful heart keeps open the door of one's life to receive even more blessings; and the second is that it is a sound bastion against the tempter's doubting voice: "I wonder if I am really any better now?"

In this period of thanksgiving the ministrant, whenever he thinks of the sufferer, will also join. Just as he prepared himself for the interview beforehand so now he gives thanks that, during it, the Lord gave His guidance and His blessing. Any thought that comes to his mind along the lines of "I wonder if he is feeling better now" is countered immediately with a "Thank You, Lord, for I know you acted in that hour, and I know that You have set into motion forces to resolve and heal that situation."

These spiritual laws are as active in our world as are the laws of gravity.

One learns very quickly not to worry about results. All we can do is to speak or touch; what is conveyed through our voices and through our hands is His. If every time we spoke in His name we began to worry about results we should very soon become inhibited in saying anything at all. We speak for Him but it is He, through the Holy Spirit, who convicts and converts. We lay hands on the sick but it is He who provides the power that heals.

In the days following the ministration the ministrant and sufferer wait trustfully for the answering manifestations of God's grace. The ministrant, in particular, will know that these will not necessarily follow an expected pattern. God's ways are not always our ways.

There will usually be an immediate easement of the trouble and sometimes a complete release from it. The sufferer will become a completely different person as God has now become very real to him. Occasionally, however, further help may be needed, usually within about three days. In some cases the pain suddenly becomes much worse. Occasionally this means that a sudden need for medical help has developed—as though the ministration has brought "to the surface" something that had been vaguely troubling the sufferer for a long time. Often the cause is what I call "the badness coming out". Usually a further ministration and a word of encouragement help him through this period; but if it doesn't he must seek his doctor's help as soon as possible. In either case, the very occasional or the more usual, we can give thanks that God has blessed the ministration for the sufferer's healing.

Again, with one who has been suffering mentally or emotionally, after about three days a set-back may occur. He feels that his old "thoughts" are returning. This is the habit-track of the mind trying to re-assert itself. Personally I think it is the devil trying to get back again! If it is explained to him that these thoughts are now ghosts of the past and that they have no longer any reality, he will put his anxieties behind him. He should be encouraged to go forward patiently in his new life while new and better habit-tracks begin to replace the old.

The effects of a ministration continue for a long while; and there is no need to worry when a set-back occurs, provided that the ministrant is sufficiently watchful to step in with a word of encouragement and perhaps also with a further "supportive" ministration.

Finally, the phrase "gradual healing" is sometimes used. Provided that the Latin derivation of the word "gradual" (step by step) is borne in mind I would agree that this has a measure of truth in it for some cases but it is not a phrase I would use. If the preparation and the interview are thorough the one ministration is usually enough to lift the sufferer from a state of dis-ease to the beginning of wholeness.

The consequences of a ministration, in terms of new attitudes and new relationships with people, may not all be worked out in a lifetime. I think of any further ministrations of the laying-on-of-hands given during the assimilative period following the main one as being simply of a "supportive" kind.

X

THREE HEALING QUALITIES

LOOKING BACK on interviews that brought great blessing, and trying to analyse the inner dispositions of the sufferers at the time, I can see three qualities whose presence appears to be vital to the power of the ministration. They are acceptance, expectant faith and surrender. They do not come all at once.

The first step towards healing is acceptance. We have to learn to accept ourselves, in God's sight, just as we are.

This may sound obvious and easy, but to some it is not. It is specially difficult to one who is deeply troubled. A sick person will often have a vague feeling of guilt and he will be searching for an answer to his questioning, "Why should this happen to me?" Sometimes he feels that he is being punished for something he has been doing or for having neglected something he ought to have done. He feels that he may have put himself "out of bounds". He feels, at least partly, cut off from God. He cannot pray as he used to do, and this seems to confirm his feelings. What he has to learn is that the experience is common to many sick people. It is a time when he can lean back on the prayers of the Church and of his friends, but he does not realise that unless someone tells him.

At other times he feels that God cannot help him because he has put himself beyond the reach of God's healing hand. He may look back to a time when he took a wrong turning and he thinks he has arrived at a place where he ought not to be. If only he had stayed on the right course, God could have helped him!

What he has to learn is whether or not he took a "wrong" turning, God allowed for it. It is not that God has only one pattern for each of us, one blue print to follow, and that if we go against His will we put ourselves beyond His reach but, rather, He has many permutations for our lives. He has made allowance for each one; wherever we may be, however far away from that wholeness which is His perfect will, it is just there, at that particular point, that He can take control. The place where the sufferer now finds himself can be a fresh starting-point on the road to God's perfect will. We can never get beyond the reach of His healing love.

Whatever the blockage may be, the sufferer must be helped to a point of acceptance, where he can realise that he can do nothing of himself, and that there is no place he can go that can put him in a better position for God to help him. He has to accept himself and his condition completely, when all he can say is a sincere, "Just as I am . . ."

At this stage there is a movement of the spirit which carries him on to the second essential quality—expectant faith.

It is clear from the gospels that expectant faith is important if any healing work is to be done. To the woman who touched the hem of His garment, Jesus said, "Thy faith hath made thee whole," and to the blind men who sought their sight He said, "According to your faith be it done unto you." Where there was faith He could heal, where it was absent He could not. In His own village, "He could do no mighty work because of their unbelief."

Sometimes He used the faith of the sufferer himself, as when blind Bartimaeus came to Him; sometimes the faith of the sufferer's friends, as when the four men carried the man sick of the palsy into His presence and He, seeing their faith, used it for the sufferer's healing. At other times He used the faith of someone closely related to the sufferer, as when Jairus came to Him on behalf of his child and when the centurion came on behalf of his servant.

On some occasions Jesus actively encouraged faith as, for example, He did when they brought a deaf-mute to Him. Jesus took him away from the crowd, spat and touched his tongue; and, again, when He reassured the father of an epileptic boy with the words, "All things are possible to him that believes."

Faith is a far more powerful quality than we shall ever know. But we can see that in the context of healing it is not simply the continuing faith of a Christian believer, however helpful that might be. It is a quality evoked for a specific occasion to meet a specific need.

This quality, when present, provides the necessary environment for an incoming of creative energy. All life is the outward manifestation of God's creative energies continuously flowing into and sustaining our created order. Where expectant faith is present the creative energies of God have free flow.

There is a significant phrase in the eleventh chapter of the Epistle to the Hebrews—"Faith is the substance of things hoped for." It suggests that faith produces an energy which can be transmuted into material form.

When the woman touched the hem of His garment she felt a movement of healing within her body. Jesus, at the same time, felt "the virtue" going out of Him. Could it be that by this "virtue" is meant the creative energies of God at work in the universe? That through this Man, who was always in perfect attunement with His Father, and by whom all things were made, flowed the very stuff of creation? I believe that this is so and that too easily have His healing works been given only a spiritual interpretation and His "nature miracles" explained away.

In my medical student days we studied the various theories of evolution. One that I remember best was called "emergent evolution". This held that at various points in history came a combination of circumstances which gave rise, in effect, to a new act of creation. A new creature came into being. I believe that in some such way as this a new act of creation enters into our human life where the quality of the environment is dominated by the presence of expectant faith. If it is present in an interview then the Lord Christ is able to supply a divine energy which He makes available for the release and healing of the sick one.

I often think that in the feeding of the five thousand we have a picture of what God can do when faith is present. Jesus asked His disciples to feed the crowd—and then come the important words, "He himself knew what He would do!" He knew what He wanted to do, what He willed to do, but He could not perform His will until the right conditions were there. At first, from His own disciples, He could get nothing but a negative response and He could do nothing with that. At long last, a child, with the faith of a child, came forward to offer the little he had.

"Master, I have five loaves here, and two small fishes. Will they do?" Now the right conditions had come. Jesus took the loaves and gave thanks. He used the faith of the child, and the little he was able to offer, to do the impossible.

Perhaps I have used a little imagination here but I think it helps to make the point that without the right conditions our Lord cannot do the things that He wants to do. Without expectant faith on our part He cannot manifest His perfect will in us. But where faith is present, there is an outpouring of creative power that can change everything.

How does expectant faith come? Certainly not by squeezing it out of ourselves. Though it is a quality latent within everyone, it cannot be switched on at a touch of a button. It has to be evoked. It comes in response to something outside of ourselves.

The whole onus of faith in an interview is on the minister or helper. It is he, because of his own knowledge of what the Christ can do and because of that other unseen conversation in which he is engaged, who should unconsciously evoke this quality. Yet, when faith comes into the interview, it comes not only to the sufferer. The minister also shares in it and both are affected by it. On the human level it is the encounter between Christian helper and sufferer which has brought it into being. On the level of the divine, it is a gift poured in by the Holy Spirit for the needs of that occasion.

A spiritual triangle has been created. The minister and the sufferer form the base and the Holy Spirit is the apex. When the triangle is made complete the atmosphere becomes vibrant with expectant faith. In such circumstances anything can happen.

At this point the interview quickly moves on to its third and final phase—an attitude, on the part of minister and sufferer alike, of complete surrender to whatever the Christ will do. As far as the minister is concerned he is ready, now, to do for the sufferer whatever the risen Christ directs. He makes no promises. He is an instrument in Christ's hands.

The sufferer now knows that he is no longer alone. His troubles have been shared and he is ready to hand them over at the feet of Christ. He is no longer asking for any particular blessing of his own choice. He is ready to accept whatever the Lord wills for him, knowing that He knows best. Whether or not he is completely healed through the ministration he knows that Christ knows and all will be well. This is not resignation; it is a glad and joyful acceptance of whatever the outcome might be.

Invariably it is something far more wonderful than anything he could have thought of himself.

XI

PUBLIC SERVICES OF HEALING

MANY PEOPLE ARE HELPED through public services of
healing. How many it is impossible to know. But one
is always hearing from men and women who have
attended such services and like to give a quiet witness to
this fact. If the story of the healing of the ten lepers is anything to go by—only one of them returned to give thanks
—many hundreds must have been helped.

Only recently I happened to be staying overnight with
an old friend who told me of a man who had suffered every
June, July and August from a recurrent bout of malaria,
and who attended one such service with his wife. At the
last moment he had decided to go up to the communion
rails to receive the laying-on-of-hands. That was two
years ago. Since then, he has been completely free from
this trouble.

Another man whom I had not seen for very many years
and whom I happened to meet recently told me that he,
too, had received a wonderful blessing through one of
these services. I remembered that he had had trouble with
his heart. He looked surprised when I asked him how the
old trouble was!

"I left that behind years ago," he said. "Don't you
remember that first service of healing we had at our

church? I've had no trouble ever since that day." I had, for the moment, forgotten the service. It had been more than ten years ago.

I received a grateful letter from a young "clergy-wife" following a mission I had been asked to conduct in the west country. She and her curate husband who walked with a limp had attended the final service of healing which concluded the mission with the special intention of asking a healing blessing for their young and backward child. They knelt side by side at the communion rails to receive the laying-on-of-hands on behalf of their child. As they got up to return to their seats and were walking down the aisle he took his wife's arm and whispered, "I can walk! The pain has gone!"

For years he had been suffering from some trouble in his lower back which often gave him spasms of great pain and caused him to limp. At the service his back was suddenly made perfect. He had even been able to take up golf again.

The following letter is typical of many. It indicates that the blessing given is something more than just a physical release.

"I want you to know how wonderfully God answered prayer last Wednesday. I first went to hospital in 1934 with an arthritic hip, and since then have had endless treatments at Droitwich and Bath, and other visits to hospitals. It spread to my other hip, knees, shoulders and neck. I could not manage without a stick and for the last few months have had much pain.

"Then I heard about the service of healing and, at the same time, I read a little leaflet of preparation which I found very helpful. The service was all so lovely—so full of peace and the presence of God. When it came to the laying-on-of-hands I did not even hear the prayer. I felt the pressure of hands on my head but it was just as if I were kneeling at Jesus' feet, and all my being was filled with wonder and peace.

"It was on the way back to my pew that I realised I was entirely free from pain and restricted movements. How humble it makes you feel—but so full of praise and thanksgiving!

"My circumstances at home are often very difficult—I needed, and had prayed for, healing of the whole person. Then, more than ever, I wanted to commit to Him all that He had made whole to be used in whatever way He wants. . . .

"I wanted to share this wonderful joy with you—God did not only give me healing, but a peace I never knew before."

Such services are spreading throughout our country nowadays—and in many other countries, too—and, as well as being channels of healing to those who go to them, they are bringing a new sense of joy and purpose to the churches where they are held. The clergy who participate in ministering the laying-on-of-hands at these services are experiencing a new awareness of the presence of Christ as they minister His healing grace in a degree which is over and above anything they have known before.

Often, a group of churches combine to arrange services of healing at regular intervals. These services are quite simple in structure. Interspersed with hymns, they consist of three parts. First, the proclamation of the healing gospel through a reading from Holy Scripture, followed by an address; second, the prayers which are offered in response to that message and these include penitence, intercession, thanksgiving and dedication; third, the laying-on-of-hands which is ministered at the communion rails.

Our Lord is upheld in the services as the great Healer above all others. They balance the private interviews in which the emphasis is inevitably on the particular need of the individual sufferer; in the services, which supply the needs of a large number of people, the emphasis is on the risen Christ.

Many people would be very hesitant to ask for help in a private interview. Either they think that their own trouble is not serious enough to warrant it, specially when compared with others with far greater problems, or they have come to accept their suffering as normal and prefer to endure in silence. Often they attend a service of healing for the main purpose of adding their prayers to those of the whole congregation and it is only on an impulse at the last moment that they feel moved to come for a blessing, too.

There are others, the neurotic and the inadequate type especially, who benefit far more from a public service of healing than from a private ministration. They have to "lose" themselves when they are surrounded by a large congregation. They are affected by the strong spiritual atmosphere created through the expectant prayers of a large body of people and this helps them to get their own sufferings in better perspective.

Perhaps it is the witness that such services give that is the most important thing about them just now. In these days when people are turning in all directions to find healing and peace, it is important that the Christian Church should be clearly seen to be preaching a gospel that has something very positive to say about sickness and disease. When the Christ is upheld in all His glory, He will draw all men unto Him. He is the divine magnet to whom men and women will turn if they are only able to *see* Him.

These services inevitably have a great effect on the prayer life of a church. If prayer groups do not already exist, the need for them is very soon felt. With a deepened prayer life the whole atmosphere of a church is changed and its worship becomes more real. A spirit of expectant faith begins to pervade all its worship and where that exists wonderful things can happen.

There are any of three reasons why we might receive the laying-on-of-hands during a service of healing.

The first is because we are conscious of having a particular need of our own for which we are seeking the healing touch of Christ. It may be physical, mental, emotional or spiritual.

Whatever it is, we can bring it confidently to Him. If it is only a physical matter we can be sure that He will understand. After all, many of those who came to Christ in the first place did so because they needed physical healing. There was blind Bartimaeus who called out to Jesus from the wayside along which He was going on His last earthly journey to Jerusalem. On such a journey one might have thought that our Lord's mind was already sufficiently engrossed to be deaf to any other calls. Evidently, His disciples thought so, too, for they told the man to be quiet. But Jesus stopped and commanded them to bring the man to Him. "What is it you want?" He asked. "Lord, that I might receive my sight," was his simple reply.

Our Lord is never too busy, *never* too preoccupied, or too high-minded to receive each one of us just as we are, and He makes the simplest physical trouble His own concern.

But there are other needs that are not so obviously physical. They may have more to do with our minds or our emotions or our souls.

The second reason why we might receive the laying-on-of-hands is that we have a burden of concern for someone or for some situation into which we want to bring Christ. This is receiving by proxy.

In my early days in the healing ministry I used to think that such a reason was unsound. With my tidy theological mind I thought that the time to bring a burden of concern to the feet of our Lord was during the time of intercession, but the facts did not work out that way. I learned in time that some of those who were coming to the communion rails for the laying-on-of-hands were doing so on behalf of someone else—and that through them a healing blessing was given. So God truly does work in mysterious ways! It is true, of course, that we can intercede for our sick friends but one has found that God does not confine the outpouring of His blessings to any particular channel.

Here is another letter. I do not know the writer.

"During the time of your address, the name of a little girl came into my mind and I felt with certainty that she was the one I must 'bring with me' and this I did. I do not know the little girl personally, but her grandmother is a friend of mine. The child had been very ill for a long time. She was unable to walk and she needed to be carried up and down the stairs and out in a wheel-chair . . .

"Her grandmother came to see me last week—she did not know about the service—and she said, 'It really is amazing! During the past three weeks, she has been walking. She even walked upstairs! . . . and she is eating better, too'."

It does not matter whether the friend or dear one knows or does not know what you are doing for them when you receive the laying-on-of-hands on their behalf. It is usually better that they do not know, otherwise they may get "all worked up" about it! Any such anxiety may well be a barrier to the flow of healing energy out-poured. It is better that they carry on with whatever they are doing in a relaxed frame of mind. Only if you are completely confident of the character of your sick friend and you have a complete rapport with him (or her) is it a help for him to know.

An old Quaker friend once told me that in the early days of the Society of Friends they used not to believe that we should pray to God about anything. It was a presumption to do so. He knew best! After a time, however, the phrase "burden of concern" entered their thinking. It had a "technical" ring about it. They came to accept that if you have a burden of concern then God has put it there as an indication that He is calling you to co-operate with Him in prayer for the healing or resolving of that situa-tion. What you had to do was to take it with you to the feet of Christ, lay it down and let it go. If you did that, utterly and faithfully, He would then set in motion forces that would overcome, heal and resolve.

The important thing was the complete handing over in expectant faith and trust. This truth applies whether or not what we bring is a burden of concern for someone else or a personal need of our own.

I shall always remember one occasion in my early days at Crowhurst where we held a service of healing every Monday evening. An old lady came to me after one of the services and told me that it seemed to hold a special message for her. I had been talking about the text,

"Nothing is impossible with God," and had spoken about handing over our troubles with complete trust.

She was deeply distressed. Some years earlier she had lost touch with her youngest son and it had been all her fault. He had made his home with her until, in the late forties, he had met and married a woman from overseas. Though it was an ideal match the mother had resented the other woman taking her son from her and she refused to go to the wedding or have anything to do with them. The couple disappeared overseas and she cut them out of her life.

As the years went by she came to realise how wrong she had been. Her first bitter resentment had long turned into remorse but there was nothing she could do about it. She longed for some sign from her son so that the broken relationship could be healed. Often she had prayed for forgiveness. She was getting old and she felt that she had not much longer to live.

I took her back into the little chapel with me and tried to think of some simple illustration which would help her hand over the deep weight of her concern to Christ. There was a large Book of Common Prayer on my desk. I picked it up and asked her to imagine that this Book represented her burden. She had told me that she had prayed night after night about it and that nothing ever seemed to happen, so I knelt down and, with arms outstretched, I held the book at the foot of the altar steps. After a long moment I got up from my knees and sat down, resting the book in my lap. Then I repeated this performance three times and asked her if that was what she did every night. "Yes," she said, "I do!"

"Well," I replied, "let us do it just once more, only this time we shall do it together and a little differently

97

from the way you have done it before. We shall do it in this way."

Again I knelt and held the book at the foot of the altar steps and after a few moments rose from my knees and sat down again. But this time the book was not on my lap. It was lying on the floor, at the foot of the altar steps.

She looked down at the book and smiled. She had taken the point and after sitting quietly for a few moments she knelt at the communion rails and in prayer we handed the whole thing over. This time she really let her burden go to the feet of Christ and did not take it back. A great sense of release and peace lit up her face.

As we were walking away from the chapel it was suddenly given me to say to the old lady, "Now that you have left it with our Lord, I have a feeling that the first signs of His answering grace will be manifested within a fortnight. Now, go to bed and give thanks."

In the days that followed it was clear that all strain and anxiety had left her. She was a happy woman once more.

There were many others to be seen and my mind soon became involved with other matters. But late one night the telephone rang. It was a long-distance call and the caller was asking if Mrs. A was staying with us. "Yes," I told him, and asked who was speaking. He told me that he was the old lady's youngest son. His work, I knew, took him all over the world and he had arrived in Edinburgh only three days before. He was due to sail away again on the next evening.

He told me that on the voyage over a strong feeling had come to him that he must get into touch with his mother; he had telephoned her home without avail and then some of her friends. None had known where she might be until

the last call he had made when he was told to try Crowhurst. I realised as he spoke and as I looked at the calendar
that it was the fourteenth day since his mother and I had
prayed together in the chapel!

He told me that he could catch a train from Edinburgh
in the early hours and could get to Crowhurst by the
early afternoon. He would be able to have about two
hours with his mother.

Next day I was on the garden path that leads to the
station when he arrived. The old lady was waiting in
her room.

I took him up to her, and I doubt if any mother had
ever known a happier day.

The third reason for receiving the laying-on-of-hands
is simply to offer oneself in surrender to our blessed Lord
for Him to do with us as He will. In this event we offer
some such simple prayer as the following, while hands are
placed on our head:

*"Lord Jesus, I may not myself be conscious of any great
need, but You who can see into the hearts of all men,
please look into mine, and cleanse and heal. I have not
much to offer but what I am and what I have I give
entirely to You. All that I ask is that You do with me as
You will, that I may become a better channel of Your
healing Love to others. Amen."*

XII

DIVINE HEALING AND MEDICINE

"GEORGE, we have a job to do! This man needs help and I think it is exorcism that he needs."

The speaker was a medical consultant and eminent in his own field. We had just got down from the platform of a crowded hall where we had been invited to speak about the Church's ministry of healing.

A minister had travelled fifty miles to this meeting, bringing with him a young man who was ill. He was under the impression that healing ministrations were to be given that night and had not realised that it was to be a public meeting only. He was very disappointed and, after the meeting was over, had worked his way to the front of the hall where the doctor and I were talking with separate groups of people. Apparently he had managed to get the doctor away from his group and had brought the young man to him.

Thus began one of many acts of co-operation I have had with members of the medical profession.

Later that evening the doctor and I stood side by side as we ministered to the young man in the side-chapel of a large nearby church which had been lent to us for the occasion by a friendly vicar. The vicar and the young man's minister knelt side by side in the front pew while we ministered to him at the communion rails. First came an act of exorcism. Then we put our hands on his head, invoking the power of the Holy Spirit to come in and give him complete healing. We heard some weeks later that he had been released from his oppression that evening and was now happy and free.

Some people believe that divine healing and medical healing are opposed and that if you are receiving help from one you ought not to seek aid from the other. This is certainly not so. It is the same God Who is behind both and Who works through both.

In the instance I have just mentioned the doctor came over to my side and took part with me in an act of divine healing. On the other hand, there have been many times when I, on my part, have advised a sufferer to seek the help of a doctor for some specific complaint. Always, when I have done so, I have asked the sufferer to regard the doctor as a minister of God, for that is what he is, whether he knows it or not.

After all, if I get a splinter in my hand I do not give it the laying-on-of-hands! I use a pair of tweezers, wash the wound and apply antiseptic. There are specific needs for which medical help is available and must be sought.

Sometimes, when ministering to a sufferer, I have sensed the need for such help. A sufferer was once sent to me by her doctor because he had been unable to locate the cause of a particular pain and thought that a ministration might relieve her. He had investigated the trouble many times but without avail. I ministered to her and she was helped, but during the course of the interview and especially while giving the ministration, I felt certain that she still needed the doctor's help. I suggested to him that the root of the trouble might be found in a particular locality. In his next investigation he found the cause of the trouble—a physical displacement—and was soon able to have it put right. This, to me, was divine healing in a wider sense.

On another occasion a doctor, with two nurses, was trying to feed by nasal tube a recalcitrant patient who was in an acutely disturbed mental state. I happened to be in the next room and the doctor sent one of the nurses to ask if I would help. The patient quietened—perhaps he was astonished to see a parson helping to hold him down!—and the doctor was able to finish his good work. Next day, that patient broke his self-imposed fast and was soon on the way to becoming completely healed.

In my own ministry I have always been fortunate in the friendships and co-operation I have enjoyed with doctors. Indeed, I often think they are more ready to accept divine healing than are many clergy! When I was a parish priest I would often discuss the needs of our people with the local doctors. Often they would say, "Half the patients who came into my surgery this morning really needed what you have to give!"

What is the relationship between Medicine and Divine Healing? The answer is that while Medicine is concerned with the cure of disease, Divine Healing is concerned with the healing of man's *whole* personality. Let us contrast the meaning of the word "cure" with the larger concept of the phrase "making whole". A cure is a specific treatment given by a doctor for a specific complaint. It provides a remedy for an illness but it cannot do more than that. Electro-convulsant-therapy, for example, can relieve a patient who has acute mental depression but it can do no more than restore him to what he was before. It cannot raise him on to a new level of life or give him a change of heart.

Divine healing lifts us above the level of the human on to

that of the divine as, through prayer and ministration, the patient is brought into that state of wholeness and perfection which can be found only in the presence of the risen Christ. And the cure of the illness troubling the patient is very often found to be incidental to the healing of his whole being.

When I was at Crowhurst I would take patients who had only just completed their psychiatric treatment. Normally, they would have stayed in hospital until they were sufficiently balanced to return home. But some of our doctor friends knew that at Crowhurst their patients would find an atmosphere of such faith and hope that they would be much better equipped to face life again than they would have been by just marking time in hospital.

I sometimes have a dream picture in my mind of a perfect healing. I see an operating theatre with doctors and nurses performing their respective roles on behalf of the patient with an awareness that God is in the midst of everything they do. Surrounding the theatre I see encircling rows of Christian people, stretching back as far as the eye can see, uplifting the whole situation into the hands of our blessed Lord, Who is the great Physician. I don't suppose such a picture could ever resemble anything in this fallen and fragmented world, but I have often ministered Holy Unction to a sufferer just before he has gone into hospital for an operation. In my prayer-intention I have included the doctors and nurses. It sets the seal of Christ upon all concerned.

Some surgeons do indeed pray before they operate. I do not think it by any means a coincidence that their patients have felt completely confident and at peace while in their hands.

But others say that they are only technicians doing a job

of work in which it does not matter what their religious beliefs might be. Even psychiatrists have sometimes been heard to voice this idea. This is sheer nonsense. For no psychiatrist can abnegate his own personality. Were he only a soulless computer he might then, indeed, be nothing more than a technician. But whether he likes it or not he is a person dealing with persons. What he is is communicated unconsciously, not so much by his words and his questions, as by the manner of them. And, as we considered earlier, a man's intuitive perception is heightened when he is sick.

So many demands are made on a psychiatrist's energies that he must keep a tight rein on his feelings by not becoming too involved. The fact remains that he cannot keep his beliefs about life in one department and his skill and technical knowledge in another.

I believe that it is largely because the Church has neglected her healing ministry that so many doctors are overworked. They are pressed to give help and advice in areas more properly belonging to the sphere of the clergy and other dedicated Christians who accept Christ's call to heal the sick. With the daily pressures of a fast-changing world and the increase in the pace of living many people are under stress and desperately need what the Church has to give. The answer to their problems is in the gospel of our Lord Jesus Christ but they cannot find it. Instead they turn to the doctor for another supply of drugs. These are no cure but, at least, they enable them to limp along with their troubles. The doctor hasn't time, even if he has the necessary qualifications, to deal with every patient as he would wish to do and he will often have to resort to handing out drugs to deaden the pain before discovering exactly what is causing it.

We have become a nation of pigs as far as drugs are concerned. We take far too many and waste far too many. Yet drugs, rightly used, are God's gift. They are the walking sticks that God provides for our use when we are going over a rough patch of ground. If I have to take a medicine I always say "grace" over it before putting it in my mouth. I like to think of it as a sacrament of God's love. Surely that is how all medicine should be seen? Just as oil and wine were the outward expressions of the Good Samaritan's concern for a wounded man, and just as the oil, with its natural healing qualities, is taken and consecrated in Holy Unction, so should all medicine be seen in this light. Medicine is a sacred thing. It is a gift of God. The psalmist puts it in its right perspective when he says, "The Lord healeth those that are broken in heart; and giveth medicine to heal their sickness."

Happy is the doctor who regards his own work in this way. In addition to his understanding of human sickness, his skills and knowledge of treatments, he knows that there is another factor—what from the narrowly scientific point of view can only be called the X factor—in the midst of all he does.

Such a doctor unconsciously integrates into his medical practice a larger view of life, a conception of Christian wholeness, and in so doing brings in this extra healing factor. Such a doctor knows that where Christ is present anything can happen and often does.

One doctor I know who is responsible for most of the confinements that come to his practice, on his first visit always holds his hand above the unborn child and asks a blessing on the new life coming into the world. It is said in his area that "all Dr. A's babies are beautiful ones!"

Another doctor, whenever I go to his part of the country to conduct a service of healing in the local church, issues invitation cards to his patients and his friends. He knows that in divine healing is a power greater than medicine. He has discovered this in his own life and ministry as a doctor and is always seeking to point his patients beyond the immediate cure to the greater healing that is to be found in Jesus, the greatest Physician of all.

Sometimes, there comes a point of tension in the relationship between medicine and divine healing. This occurs when the sufferer has been relying on drugs for a long time and is then suddenly confronted with a vision of a more victorious life lived without their aid. This may happen during a service of healing or at one of the other services; or when he finds himself in an atmosphere of Christian love, or in response to the faithful prayers of friends. "The kingdom of God has come nigh unto" him. He suddenly sees the drugs for what they have become to him. No longer are they friendly walking sticks provided by a merciful Lord to help him temporarily. He has allowed them to become part of himself. They are limbs! He is brought to a point of decision. Can he now cast all his care upon God in utter faith that He will carry him through to perfect wholeness or must he forever rely on the props that drugs afford? I have often seen this tension in a sufferer's mind and it has been good to help him take a leap of faith and leave his drugs behind.

Fortunately, the kind of doctor I have mentioned understands this situation. At Crowhurst I used to hand to the doctor a collection of drugs left behind by sufferers no longer needing them. They matched the slowly growing number of walking sticks that were left in the front hall.

A question often asked is: Can divine healing do anything about incurable illnesses? The answer is *yes*. Divine healing knows no incurable illness. Doctors use the word "incurable" to define illnesses for which as yet no cure has been found. Twenty-five years ago the list of incurable illnesses was much longer than it is today and, please God, it will have shrunk considerably, if not altogether, in another twenty-five years. Is the power of God restricted to the list of yesteryear? Or this year? Or any year? His power is not limited by any list composed at any particular time by medical science.

In divine healing it is not so much that there are incurable illnesses as incurable people! There are those who will not listen, who will not believe. It is as though, having ears, they cannot hear, and, having eyes, they cannot see. There was the occasion when Jesus asked a sufferer who had lain by the pool of Bethesda many years, waiting for someone to push him in—or so he said!—"Do you want to be healed?" It was a telling question then and it is a telling question still to some sufferers today; for to be healed would involve them in taking up responsibilities from which they shrink.

There does, however, seem to be one particular barrier to divine healing which might be termed incurable. Sometimes when ministering to a sufferer one detects a "deadness" in one part of the body which does not respond. It is sometimes due to a mistake having been made in an operation or by over-treatment. Years ago I ministered to a woman who had cancer round her face and neck. She was in a piteous condition but had accepted it bravely and really came for a ministration as a preparation for her coming death.

I was surprised to meet her again some months later. It

was after a service of healing in a city church. I was standing near the door as people went out. Suddenly, among them, was this woman. She greeted me very happily and told me that the cancer had gone. Certainly her face looked more normal and the skin had healed, but she told me she was having great difficulty in digesting her food. I heard later that she died, not from the cancer but from the radium treatment. It had done too much damage.

It is vital, however, that we keep our minds completely open. If we close them by saying—or even believing—that someone has an incurable disease, we help to make it so. We help to fasten the illness more tightly on to him. But if we believe that "with God all things are possible" we hold the door open to God's incoming grace, and sometimes the "impossible" happens.

Some years ago I was conducting a healing mission for a group of parishes near the Welsh border. During the mission there was a meeting for clergy and ministers only, and we discussed the problem of how best we could help those with "incurable" illnesses. It was generally agreed that given a sound Christian faith the sufferer could, in effect, overcome the disease and find wholeness on a deeper level. One or two present cited examples of people in their own parishes who had wonderfully overcome their troubles and were among the most Christlike people they knew.

After the meeting, one of the clergy told me of such a woman who lived on the edge of his parish. She was something of a saint and was praying continually for the mission even though she could not attend any of the meetings herself. Her great desire was that many in that area would be blessed. He took me to see her that afternoon.

On the way there he told me she was about sixty-four and when she was four years old she was stricken with an illness which the doctors now thought must have been polio. Ever since, she had lived in the same tiny cottage and was now quite alone. Many friends called to see her, to help her from her bed to her chair each morning and to clean up and make a pot of tea.

We had travelled four or five miles from his vicarage by the time he stopped his car at the roadside. We got out and walked a hundred yards or so down a rutted lane. There were two cottages, both facing down the valley to our right. On our left was a tall hedge, behind which the hill rose steeply. The far cottage was tumble-down but the near one was obviously inhabited and where she lived.

Her front door was wide open and the sun was streaming in. The vicar got there just a little ahead of me and I saw his face fall. "Hello," he said, "is it hurting this afternoon?" I did not hear her reply but as I went in there were tears falling down her cheeks. She smiled, however, and welcomed us.

It was only a tiny room and the vicar sat opposite her while I sat on a small stool between her and the fireplace. For a while the two talked together and then there was a silence. Suddenly, I found myself turning to her and asking if I could lay my hands on her. She seemed to understand and nodded. As I got up from my stool the vicar bowed his head in prayer and so did she. I remember holding my hand for some moments near the base of her back, knowing and feeling the healing love of Christ flowing through. In my right forearm there came a great pain which persisted for nearly three days. "Now put your right foot to the ground," I told her, "and now your left," and she did so. "Now, stand up, for we are going for a walk."

In complete silence, with the vicar taking her left arm and I her right, we walked out of the cottage and for about twenty-five yards up that rutted lane. When we turned round we saw that some cows had come out of a field but we got back to the cottage before they reached us.

After a little time of thanksgiving and prayer we left her, the vicar promising to return next day to take her for another walk.

We drove back without a word passing between us, but when we were half-way back to his vicarage, the vicar drew into the side of the road. After a few moments, he said, "This woman, whom Satan hath bound these sixty years!" He switched on the engine and drove on.

I make no comment except to say that the vicar and I shared together in a vivid consciousness of Christ's presence in that tiny room and that we had witnessed a wonderful manifestation of God's glory.

Since that day I have learned never to close doors against the wonders that God can do. Even if a person is stricken down with the most terrible of illnesses, one can never know what the issue might be if God is there. To keep our hearts open, for the sake of the sufferer and for the sake of the Kingdom, to the incoming creative energies of God's healing love is all that He asks us to do. It is more than enough!

I thank God for the medical help that He has sent into this world. I thank God for my own doctor who is always ready to assist me when I need his help. I thank God for my dentist and for the nurses who play their part in the grand design of His healing purposes. Most of all and through them all I thank God for His Son, Jesus Christ, who gives so freely of that deep and perfect healing which goes to the very heart of me—the healing which, through His sharing with us in our sins and sicknesses, He has made available to all who believe and put their trust in Him.

XIII

A LADDER INTO REALITY

MANY PRAYER GROUPS for the healing of the sick have come into existence over the past few decades and hardly a day goes by without a new one being formed. Moved by the Holy Spirit they are part and parcel of the Church's recovery of her healing ministry and they provide the basis of all our healing work. Some are linked with the Guild of Health, the Divine Healing Mission or the Guild of St. Raphael or with one of the other Healing Societies in the Church, from whose headquarters* helpful booklets giving guidance to prayer groups can be obtained. All are concerned with the recovery of the healing ministry as a normal and integral part of the life of the local church to which the members belong.

They do not all originate in response to a call put out by the vicar or minister for one to be formed in his parish; many come spontaneously into being because someone felt deeply moved by the Spirit to mention to a friend that this was something he or she felt they ought to be doing.

*Guild of Health, Edward Wilson House, 26, Queen Anne Street, London, W.1.
Divine Healing Mission, The Old Rectory, Crowhurst, Nr. Battle, Sussex.
Guild of St. Raphael, 77, Kinnerton Street, London, S.W.1.

Some of these groups are quite small in number—literally just "two or three gathered together in His name"—while others are much larger. It has been found that when a group numbers more than a dozen it is time to think of splitting into smaller groups.

Some years ago a friend of mine, then the managing director of a large motor-car factory, told me that he had found that a meeting of a dozen people could produce results where a much larger meeting would have floundered. It was a factory with a very sound and happy team-spirit and was extraordinarily free of strikes. Every week he held meetings with the shop-stewards but he always saw to it that they met in groups of not more than twelve at a time. He told me that at a managers' conference held at one of the colleges at Oxford, they had been discussing this phenomenon and, at the luncheon break, they had been invited by the Dean to look out on to the quadrangle from his balcony. They watched the undergraduates as they rushed from the lecture rooms and gathered in informal groups. It was interesting, he said, to watch how these groups grew in number. But each time they exceeded a dozen they soon split up into smaller groups. My friend concluded with a smile, "The Master chose twelve, didn't He? He knew more about psychology than the rest of us!"

The important thing about prayer groups is that they develop a group mind, that the individual members become one in Christ, bound together by the Spirit of the Living God. Power is engendered when they do. It is interesting to recall the unity which developed among the first disciples before the day of Pentecost. They continued steadfastly together in prayer and, on the day that the Holy Spirit was outpoured upon them in power, they "were all with one accord in one place". This same law is touched upon by our Lord when He speaks of the two or three gathered together in His name. "If two of you shall agree on earth as touching anything that they shall ask, it shall be done for them of my Father which is in heaven." Furthermore, I think that when our Lord promises to be "in the midst" He means not only that His risen Self comes to join them but that He is also, to coin a word, in the very "midstness" of the gathering. In a sense, then, the group at prayer becomes the body of Christ Himself.

In this way we find what is meant by "the power of prayer". Yet it is not the group that originates the power, nor the prayer alone. The power is the very energies of God upholding the universe and becoming focalised for His use and glory in the group. What prayer has done is to fling open the doors to His incoming power that His will might be done on earth as it is in heaven.

Into this situation we bring our burdens of concern, the sick and the troubled who have asked us to pray for them, the places of discord in home and church and national life and all the dis-ease of our fallen world.

There are two methods of prayer generally used and each group has to discover by experience which suits it the better, though some groups will happily and with advantage use both.

One is known as intercession, the other as contemplative meditation. They are complementary aspects of the same thing—the asking for, and the receiving of, God's gift of healing and wholeness. In the transfer of any gift there are two sides—the act of giving and that of receiving. There is a grace of giving and a grace of receiving. Both are essential, and can be seen in such a passage from Holy Scripture as

Matthew 7: 7–12, which begins with our Lord's invitation, "Ask, and it shall be given you; seek, and ye shall find; knock, and it shall be opened unto you." It ends with His assurance, "How much more shall your Father which is in heaven give good things to them that ask Him."

The one method emphasises the asking and the other emphasises the receiving.

Intercession is asking. It is usually based on the pattern of the healing of the man who was sick of the palsy (Mark 2: 1–12). Four friends agree together to give their time and energies in carrying a man who is sick into the presence of Jesus. They have a journey to make, obstacles to overcome and a burden to carry. When they arrive they carry him into our Lord's presence and He, "seeing *their* faith", uses it for the healing of the man. His healing is complete; He gives him not simply a cure of the physical illness but a cleansing and forgiving of his sins. Our Lord is concerned with our wholeness.

This kind of praying uses our imagination. Imagination is a gift common to all and it reaches its highest point when it is used in prayer. Imagination is the ladder up which we climb into reality. As we join ourselves together in intercession we "climb" into the presence of the risen Christ and having reached this reality the ladder is no longer needed. It has done its good work and can be kicked away.

Again, we use our imagination as we "see" the illness giving way under the touch of Christ and the person for whom we pray being filled with the wholeness which is God's perfect will for him. We hold on to this picture and when the meeting is over and we have returned home we shall continue to "see" him in that way.

In contemplative meditation the emphasis is on our receiving. We know that God's will is our perfection and we receive and claim that perfection by dwelling on it. Usually a phrase based on Scriptural truths is taken. For example, "My peace pervades your whole being." We know that God's peace is not simply an absence of strife, but that it is something much more positive. We know that our Lord conferred on his disciples a peace which is not "as the world giveth", and that it has to do with the fruit of the Spirit. But we do not spend a lot of time considering what we think it might mean but rather we take the selected phrase and let it speak for itself. We let God use it to speak to us in the very depths of our being as we go into silent meditation on the phrase. When its truth has permeated our inner-self we arrive at a stage when we can take into our hearts those for whom we pray. We hold them close to us so that the experience of the meditation can be shared with them.

There is a third method which I often use privately and also in leading a group in prayer. It is often called "absent healing". It means our travelling in the Spirit to the room or bedside of someone for whom we have been called to pray. But we cannot do that immediately we enter into prayer lest it become simply a psychic projection of our own energies. First, we must relax completely in God.

I think that real prayer does not begin until after all the immediate needs of our souls are first satisfied. When we come to God we are at first conscious of many needs, and not least our own pressing need for His forgiving and cleansing. His Spirit has to overcome such barriers in us before we can be at peace. As St. Augustine said, "Our hearts are restless till they rest in Thee." Then there are all the thanksgivings we want to make for His mercies and the recollections of His grace at work in the lives of our loved ones and friends. Many voices press on us and have to die away. It takes time to enter into the deep places of prayer.

It is only when all these have passed and we begin to relax into His pervading presence that we enter fully into the world we call prayer. We can then begin to come into harmony with all creation and we find the sweet companionship of angelic beings and the smile of heaven. We listen as He speaks silently to us. Here we enter into an attunement with God in which our souls are free. Here we find not so much a striving as an accepting: here there is no attempt to change the course of God's will but a joyful acceptance of it.

It is then, when we abide and relax in Him, guarded by His Spirit and filled with Christ's love, that we can go and "visit" our friend. We arrive in his room and we watch the surrounding peace and joy of heaven enter him. Sometimes we hold our hands in blessing over him; then, after a little while, we return to abide once again in the Father.

We should humbly and gratefully thank God that He uses this method. Among many messages I have had was one from the father of a young man lying critically ill in hospital. The doctors had done all they possibly could for him. There was nothing more that they or anybody could do. Suddenly, the young man came out of a deep sleep, feeling better. He told his father that during the night I had come to give him the laying-on-of-hands. The power, he said, had unmistakably flowed through his whole body. His father and I had prayed for him the night before. It was the turning point on his road to health.

So prayer, whatever form it takes, is the greatest power in the world. Through prayer men are healed, saved, and born anew. In prayer we enter for awhile into the ceaseless movement of God's creative activity. In prayer we abide in the real but unseen world, for what is of significance in the world in which we live is but the outward expression of that which is within.

Prayer is not just the odd ten minutes or so we spend on our knees. It is a continuing conversation through each and every day. It is a continuing awareness of the movement of the Holy Spirit, especially in the lives of those we meet. Prayer is an aligning of our wills with the divine will, a uniting with Him as He seeks to bring His kingdom to us. Without prayer we begin to die.

Our Lord often told His disciples to pray. Five times in the intimacy of the Upper Room on the night He was betrayed, He encouraged them to bring their requests to the Father. "Ask," He said, "and you will receive, that your joy might be full" (John. Chs. 13–16).

They knew that prayer played a prominent part in His own life. They had known the times when He had gone away from them, sometimes into the hills, to spend long hours in prayer with the Father and they had realised how vital these moments were to Him and how fundamental they were to His life and ministry. "Lord, teach us to pray," they had asked Him earlier. In response He had given them that perfect pattern of all prayer which we call the Lord's Prayer.

His had been the most active life the world has ever seen, yet He was never "busy". There was never any wasted effort, never any sense of hurry. He was always in perfect control. Somebody once called Him the greatest master of conversation who has ever lived. All that He said was perfect. There was never a word too many, nor one too few. And the words He spoke still continue to ring through the ages. We have not outlived them yet.

It was also the same with everything He did. All His actions were perfect. Never, when a sufferer came to Him for help, was there any "demonstration of healing" When they brought to Him a man who had been born deaf and dumb He quietly took him aside from the crowd and set the man at ease as He touched his ears and put spittle on his tongue, releasing him from his trouble. When He lifted the child up from her sick bed and restored her to her parents, He was thoughtful enough to say: "Give her something to eat."

Those three years of His earthly ministry have made a bigger impact on the whole course of history than any number of years in the life of any other man. And behind it all was prayer.

How did He pray? What method did He use? The questions seem almost pointless and impious. It was a simple abiding in the Father, a resting in the limitless resources of God's creative energies, a replenishing of divine power for His daily needs and for the needs of others. Prayer was His daily bread.

As He commissions us to continue His work, so does He know that it cannot be done in any other way than the way He did it. Without prayer there is no healing, for without prayer there is no life. "I speak not from myself," He said, "but the Father abiding in me doeth His works."

Prayer is an entering with Him into the eternal flow of conversation that God has with all mankind and, indeed, with all that He has made. Earlier, when we were considering the manner of a private interview, we thought of the minister holding a two-way conversation, one with the sufferer and the other with the risen Christ. Prayer is this other conversation. It is the God-given avenue for His forgiving and creative and healing energies to enter into the world. It springs from a coming into perfect attunement with the Source of all creation. It is the effective realisation of the attunement made possible by Christ between man and his Creator.

It was this perfect attunement in a continuing conversation with His Father that was the supreme mark of Jesus and from which all His saving and His healing work flowed. He wants us to enjoy this conversation, for it is only from this source that there comes any real significance in anything that we say or do. We cannot fashion the kingdom of God on earth by our own thinking and planning, however clever or devoted our hearts and minds may be.

He made this clear in the parable of the vine and the branches. "As the branch cannot bear fruit of itself, except it abide in the vine, so neither can ye, except ye abide in me." Healing is not simply the release from physical suffering but the fruit of life as it is lived abundantly in Him. Healing comes into our imperfect world as an expression of that perfect life which He has for each one of us in heaven. It is life lived in His kingdom.

He goes on to say, "If ye abide in me and my words abide in you, then ask what you will . . ." Even our requests, then, are motivated not so much by our own ideas of how we think things ought to be, but rather as they are inspired in us by the Holy Spirit as we abide in Him. In short, He Himself will provide us with the burdens that He wants us to bring to Him. He will supply us with the people He wants us to pray for. As we enter into an attunement with Him, He will bring into our minds and hearts the things He wants us to lift into His presence. This, I think, is what He means by praying "in His name".

The heart of healing is found in prayer through which we come into the presence of the risen Christ and find our home in Him.

XIV

THE WAY INTO LIFE

CAN YOU IMAGINE a life which is perfect in every stage from birth, through childhood and adolescence to full maturity, and then beyond to the declining years where death, with its release of the spirit, is the most natural thing in all the world? If you can, you will be getting a glimpse of how God ultimately wills it to be. He has designed the span of our earthly years in just this way and He sees this design, as He sees everything that He has made, as being very good.

Sickness can strike at any time but, thanks be to God, the power of the risen Christ to heal and transform is always available. He came that we might have Life, and have it more abundantly. I have had the privilege of ministering to people of all ages, but the highest privilege of all has been to minister to those whose earthly days are nearly over.

Even when they are unconscious the healing power of Christ gets through to them. When ministering at this late stage of their journey, I find it is best to speak clearly and slowly close to their ear, and to use well-known words and phrases. A few verses from the twenty-third Psalm or from the fourteenth chapter of St. John's Gospel and, of course, the Lord's Prayer, always penetrate their unconscious state and give comfort, reassurance and peace. The laying-on-of-hands or Holy Unction can also be given so that the creative energies of God's healing love will pour in.

The Christian sees our earthly life against the back-cloth of a far more wonderful life destined for us and which, through prayer, we can experience to some extent here. It is to the unseen world that we ultimately belong.

Christian teaching sees our life in three stages. First, there is the earthly life of "three score years and ten"; then the second or intermediate stage which we often call Paradise; and finally, the consummation of all things in heaven, heralded by what St. Paul calls "the day of the Lord" and which we acknowledge in our Creed as being brought into being "when He shall come again in glory to judge both the quick and the dead".

Paradise is the descriptive word used by our Lord when He spoke to the thief on the cross. It means park-land, or beautiful garden. It seems to restore again the theme of the Garden of Eden which, in picture form, reminds us of that perfect life in which we had our origin.

Often I have heard someone who has reached the borderland between this life and the next say that he has glimpsed a beautiful garden, full of the most colourful flowers he has ever seen. I think this is how our earthly mind interprets the vision of Paradise. Sometimes there is the presence of a loved one, who has gone that way before, standing beside the bed as if in welcome. Trying honestly to assess whether or not what has been seen has been real or only an hallucination, I cannot help but feel that a moment of clarity, which we cannot know, has been given to those who are passing on.

I often think that when we are deeply moved by beauty, truth or goodness we have a glimpse of the other life that awaits us. It is as if something within us is recognising what we have known and lost awhile. It is like an echo from a distant shore. However materially minded we may have become we still have a chord within us which responds to the soul of music, poetry and all other lovely things. They take us beyond the boundaries of the material world into the limitless unseen where Christ dwells eternally.

Jesus told us not to be troubled about the life beyond but to put our trust entirely in Him. Wherever we may be and whatever our condition, we are always in His Father's House, which stretches through time to eternity. In His Father's House are many "mansions". The word Jesus used means resting-places. Our risen Lord, Who has overcome all evil, goes ahead to prepare a place for us.

A vision of the more abundant life, free from the ravages of sin and sickness, is given by St. John the Divine: "They shall hunger no more, neither thirst any more; neither shall the sun light on them, nor any heat. For the Lamb which is in the midst of the throne shall feed them, and shall lead them unto living fountains of waters: and God shall wipe away all tears from their eyes" (Rev. 7: 16–17 A.V.).

So the Christian concerned with the healing aspect of the gospel never seeks to change the ordering of God's perfect pattern. He accepts each stage of life as it comes and he knows that whether it be in childhood or in old age the power of the risen Christ to heal and transform is always available through those who believe. Through the power of His victory over all evil, life can have its perfect beginning and its perfect end. The Christian healer does not offer a rejuvenating pill that will condemn people to live here for ever!

The Christian sees our sufferings in a far more wonderful setting than in that part of it which is lived here on earth. He knows, too, that when illness has become so widespread in a human body that it can no longer provide a fit temple for the spirit, even this situation can be transformed by the ever-present living Christ. The Christian then prays confidently with the sufferer and sees the evil relinquishing its power to its Conqueror. The kingdom of our blessed Lord comes into the situation and the Holy Spirit pours out His love, joy and peace. Paradise is, indeed, already beginning.

Jesus told us that we already knew the way the journey to Paradise would take. We could find it as we became identified with Him.

When He became incarnate He recapitulated within His own earthly life the whole of the evolutionary process, just as does every man born into this world. He gathered into Himself all of creation and in doing so He brought everything that God has made into the field of His gospel of redemption. He reached beyond the level which ordinary man can attain and into the final perfection of our manhood. It is in Him and through Him that our perfection is to be found and our divinely willed destiny ultimately fulfilled.

The heart of healing is in the heart of the gospel; and the heart of the gospel is the victory of Christ.